SQUASH THE BEEF

And Accept Your Path and Purpose.

Accepting Where I Belong

Terrell Jabbarr

Squash the Beef
And Accept your Path & Purpose

Accepting Where I Belong

First Edition

Ⓞ **Chef.terrelljabbarr**

"When you don't feel like you are all the way put together, anyone will do."

-Dr. B, EdD, LPC, CPCS, SAP

TABLE OF CONTENTS

Preface: Longing to *Belong*
Prologue: *A Hungry Child Can not Learn*

TABLE OF CONTENTS CONTINUED

SQUASH THE BEEF

Accepting Where I Belong

LONGING TO BELONG
PREFACE

1 Peter 2:9
But ye are a chosen generation, a royal priesthood, a holy nation, a peculiar people; that ye should shew forth the praises of him who hath called you out of darkness into his marvelous light.

This morning, after my prayer, The Creator revealed a truth that I didn't like. He said: You always longed to belong, often yearning to belong where you didn't belong.

Although painful, it was correct. I have always yearned to fit into relationships, groups, or organizations (even now as an adult). I was always peculiar and distinctive and belly-ached to belong. I'd bend, contort, and dumb myself down to fit in, only to find myself betrayed, uncomfortable, disappointed, feeling out of place, and left embarking on another lonely search for that elusive place of belonging.

Then, however, my head spun when God went on to say: But I put that longing in you. Everything around you is made to support your purpose. Everything! Even you longing to belong. It has its purpose. It's your catalyst.

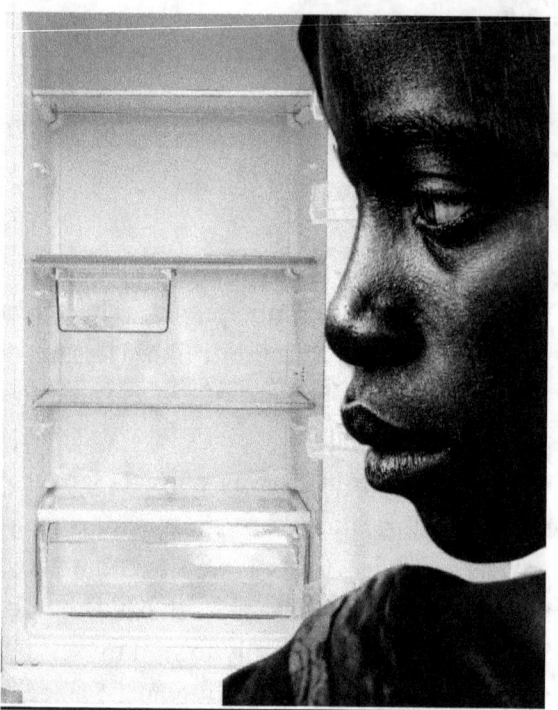

Empty

Isaiah 41:17
When the poor and needy seek water, and there is none, and
their tongue is parched with thirst, I the Lord will answer them;
I the God of Israel will not forsake them.

A HUNGRY CHILD CAN NOT LEARN

I recall stealing socks off the neighbor's clothesline at night because I had none. Growing up in the small section 8 project housing development in Wilmington, Delaware, my brothers and I stayed running the streets and stealing food from the local grocery stores to eat. I remember breaking into the Penny-candy Lady's house to steal Boston baked beans, sunflower seeds, Lemonheads, and her TV. She never knew who did it. It broke her heart, as it did mine. Mrs. Crisby was a loving elder who only gave back to the community. That's why it tore me to pieces. But I was ten, foolish, and a hungry child who, on many days, school lunch and breakfast were my only decent meals.

Rolling Stones

My mom, Norma Jean Wilson, a thin, beautiful, light-skinned woman, dropped out of Middle school at age fifteen when she began giving birth to my brothers and me

0

sequentially, one every year, starting in 1967. I was the youngest of the five boys, Terrell Wilson, Rells for short. With three fathers between us, two fathers were rolling stones; they got ghost. The third one, my father, was murdered when I was two. One of his side-chicks had a jealous boyfriend who plunged a knife into his heart. The story terrified me so much that throughout my childhood, I was petrified of girls with boyfriends, even platonic ones. I didn't want to be stabbed to death by a jealous boyfriend. I may have appeared shy around the girls, but the truth is, I was paralyzed with the fear of death.

My Mom attempted to return to school to better herself, but it was futile. Raising five boys as a single mom, working long hours, and spending countless hours at the hospital with Grandmom and my oldest brother was too much to balance. Grandmom was battling cancer, while my oldest brother, Bear, was severely asthmatic. Bear and Grandmom were often in the same hospital at the same time. He was on one floor while Grandmom was on another. Mom had to hustle between the two.

Attending to Grandmom, Bear, and work was too much for Mom. The school had to go.

Crumb-pickers

The other brothers and I, whom Grandmom called Crumb-pickers, ran the streets all day and stole groceries

1

from the local convenience stores. Grandmom was right. We were thieving little crumb-pickers, just surviving to eat.

If we weren't running the streets and stealing food, Mom had us attending mandatory church, sometimes three times a week. She had found Christ after her best friend had given her a marijuana joint and not told her it was laced with embalming fluid. Mom hallucinated for three days, seeing a short three-foot Tin man following her around. When she came through the hallucinations, she had given her life over to Christ, a promise to God if He brought her back to sanity. Thankfully so. Some drugs people don't come back from, mentally or physically.

The Crumb-pickers hated church, as did Grandmom. She thought Pastor Koonce, a slicked-haired, crooning reverend who drove a new cream-colored Cadillac Seville, was hustling Mom for her tithes. The Crumb-pickers hated it because we couldn't run the streets on Sunday and were labeled as Sister Norma's five hard-headed boys.

Mom attended anyway, fulfilling her promise to God. Mom also thought that church would deter our thieving ways. Nope! The Crumb-pickers would sneak out of the church during prayer, walk to 7-Eleven, rob them blind of sandwiches and snacks, and return to church before anyone noticed. Our middle brother, Oats, the self-proclaimed preacher of the family, preached that we would burn in hell for leaving church and stealing. So, my

2

brother Larry, believing hell was hot, began stealing cold sodas –a cold beverage might help with the heat of hell. So much for the saying, 'A hungry child cannot learn.' Our hunger led us to learn how to rob, steal to eat, and even rob the Penny-candy lady.

Hoop dreams

In the summer of 1985, as high school approached, I saw hoops as my way out of the hood. One of my childhood brothers, Eric Blackiston, and I spent countless hours at Eden Park practicing our left-hand lay-up and cross-over handle with a tennis ball. Like Terence Stansbury of the Indiana Pacers, we were determined to be the next Delawarians to go to the NBA. We used to watch Terence mastering his iconic Statue of Liberty dunk in Eden Park, the dunk he debuted in the 1985 NBA Dunk contest.

Eric was a big eleven-year-old who got fouled hard on the playground because he was huge for his age. He'd whine but eventually toughened up after playing our version of free, also called 32. It was a half-court, free-for-all game that went to 32. The person in last place got kicked in the butt by everyone. This created a champion-ship atmosphere, with everyone hustling, scrapping, re-bounding, elbowing, and shoving. The humiliation of be-ing kicked in the butt was an excellent motivator. Of course, a few runners bolted after losing, but we caught them and kicked them extra hard for running. By age

3

fifteen, Eric was balling strong with the older boys, dunking hard on them, taking, and giving hard fouls, and kicking their butts, literally.

Eric attended Mt. Pleasant, but I wanted to attend Newark High. But my second oldest brother, Moses, during a collect call from prison, assured me that I, standing at five feet, seven inches, would never make that championship team that Terence Stansbury once attended. He urged me to attend Hodgson Vocational Technical High School and take up Culinary Arts as he had done when he'd attended six years earlier. But why should I take up cooking when I had no passion for it? Moses assured me that I'd never be hungry again.

Street life

Although Moses was quick-witted and book-smart, he never pursued cooking after high school and sadly opted for a life on the streets. He spent most of my middle and high School years going in and out of Gander Hill prison. When he was out, Mom ensured we didn't let him in the house when she was at work or visiting Grandmom or Bear at the hospital. If the Wilmington Housing Authority found out a tenant was arrested for drugs, the entire family would be put on the streets with their belongings. We had to lock the doors and windows, ensuring he didn't get in. God forbid if you were home when he came knocking. His relentless banging on the door and constant yelling out your name for you to open the door were agonizing.

"YO, RELLS! RELLS! I KNOW YOU'RE IN THERE! OPEN THE DOOR"!

I'd turn off the TV, staying motionless until he drifted away, waiting an additional five minutes to be sure he was gone. I understood his dilemma. After all night on the streets, he needed a place to crash and eat, but I never wanted to be put out on the streets. Even sadder is that I began selling cocaine while he was in prison.

The come-up.

My cocaine-dealing days lasted only a few weekends. I was sixteen then, and another of my childhood brothers, Beloff, guided me away from that foolishness. This wasn't the first time he had to school me. The first time was after I robbed the Penny Candy lady when I was ten. Being three years older than me, he schooled me on my wrongdoing. We've been brothers ever since.

After I shared with Beloff that a dealer had given me an ounce of raw cocaine to hold. Beloff snapped! I was taking all the risk and jeopardizing my entire family. Beloff immediately told me to return that stuff –but not before we taxed it. We sold enough to COME UP and handed back the drug dealer some shake (that's a smidgen of what he gave me) as repercussions for trying to take

5

advantage of me. The dealer didn't get mad; Beloff scolded him.

Hand-me-down

I needed the come-up. I was tired of being called Hand-me-down, a nickname given to me throughout middle school by a few classmates who recognized me wearing the same clothes handed down to me by Moses. However, my drug sales now allowed me to buy fresh gear, haircuts, a name belt that read RELLS, a temporary gold tooth grill, and Jordan 3s. I was the freshest thing going back to school. Back to that saying, '*A hungry child can't learn.*' I learned to sell drugs. Thank God my brother Beloff guided me away from that nonsense.

Off to college

Although Moses guided me to take culinary arts because I was a hungry child, God had additional plans. My Culinary Instructor, Mr. James Mullins, a navy-bred Irishman, took me under his wing, taught me much about humility, and got me a scholarship to attend Johnson & Wales University in Providence, Rhode Island, the same City that Eric would be going. He'd attend Brown University after leading Mt. Pleasant to a state championship, becoming First Team and All-State. We hadn't planned that. It just happened.

CHAPTER 1
A PIECE OF THE PIE

- **MOVING ON UP**

2 Corinthians 9:8
And God is able to bless you abundantly, so that in all things
at all times, having all that you need, you will abound in every
good work.

MOVING ON UP

Strangely, in the Projects or Section 8, the more you earn, the more you pay —and the fewer food stamps you get. Mom, wanting to better herself, had a good job and great pay, and so was paying nearly $400.00 a month for the same dilapidated project dwelling that our neighbors were paying $20.00 a month for —and they were getting food stamps. Mom's food stamps were cut off because she earned too much. The system is backward. The incentive appears to be: Don't work, don't better yourself, pay less rent, and collect food stamps, or we'll tax the hell out of you when you try to better yourself. Mom's options were to continue giving $400.00 to Section 8 or buy a home. Having faith in God *and financial literacy*, Mom was moving out of the projects.

The Eastside

Mom had purchased her first home on the East side, an appealing historic district with rich heritage encapsulated in architectural charm. She used to always say, "I can't

8

have nothing with you children around!" She was right. It took the other Crumb-Pickers to leave before she got anything good. Moses was incarcerated then, and I was the last one staying in the new home during my last year of high school while planning to attend college.

I was happy for Mom; I could feel her sense of accomplishment resonating deep inside her. She was *also* a *peculiar people*, probably where I inherited it from. She always knew the projects weren't where she belonged.

I, too, was thankful. No more groups of crack addicts, hustlers, and dice throwers boisterously huddled outside my window from 2:00-3:00 in the morning while I was trying to get some sleep for school. And I was thankful because the school bus was now picking me up on the East side, in front of homes with architectural charm. No more stench of pissy brick walls the following day. What a come-up! I was no longer Hand-me-down. I was now Middle-class. However, I never felt like I genuinely belonged with my middle-class peers at school. They often teased and shunned me for being from the projects. But now, finally, I get a little retribution. Although I was no longer in the PJs, the projects were still in me. It was time for them middle-class bastards to get the middle finger and eat humble pie. I was off to college in June *like they were not*. Deuces, you middle-class bums.

HUMBLE SWEET POTATO PIE
YIELD: 8. PREP TIME: 15 MIN. COOK TIME: 1 HR 45 MIN.

INGREDIENTS:
3 cups sweet potato, skinned & cut into chunks.
4 cups Orange Juice
1 cup water
½ cup softened butter
1 cup white sugar
½ cup milk
2 large eggs
½ teaspoon ground nutmeg
½ teaspoon ground cinnamon
½ teaspoon ground ginger
One teaspoon of vanilla extract
1 (9 inch) Graham cracker pie crust

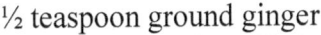

DIRECTIONS: Preheat the oven to 350 degrees F
Cover cut sweet potatoes in a pot of orange juice and water and bring to a simmer. Simmer until tender when pierced with a fork, 30 to 40 minutes.
Remove the sweet potato from the pot, drain it, and place it in a bowl. Add the butter and mix with an electric mixer until well combined.
Add sugar, milk, eggs, nutmeg, cinnamon, ginger, and vanilla; beat on medium speed until smooth.
Pour filling into unbaked Graham cracker pie crust. Bake in the preheated oven until a knife inserted in the center comes out clean, 55 to 60 minutes.

CHAPTER 2

Chef Bro-Ardee

- **CHEF BRO-ARDEE**
- **CAREMELLO BABES**
- **BEAUTIFUL**

Proverbs 17:17
A friend loves at all times, and a Brother is born for a time of adversity.

CHEF BRO-ARDEE

When I was growing up, there were only a few cooking shows on PBS: Julia Child, the well-known American French chef; Martin Yan, the beloved Hong Kong-American chef; and Justin Wilson, the humorist Southern American Chef from Louisiana who "Garontee" his meal and glass of wine was always delicious.

Now, however, cooking is a big deal, boasting entire networks dedicated to just food, multiple cooking competition shows, and celebrity chefs from across the globe. I've met a few celebrity chefs, and to my surprise, they have agents like sports and Hollywood stars. It was no wonder why the culinary campus of Johnson & Wales University during my Freshman year was buzzing with students from all walks of life, races, colors, and creeds professionally dressed in tall, white, pleated chef hats, neckerchiefs, checkered black chef pants, and black, high-glossed-polished skid-proof shoes.

I felt somewhat guilty. While most students were there with the determination to be a world-class Michelin-starred chef or the next celebrity cooking star, culinary wasn't my passion. I was just happy to get out of the Projects and eat.

Johnson & Wales was a small college in the looming shadow of the towering Brown University campus. Although Johnson & Wales offered other majors like fashion, paralegal, and equestrian, culinary was its crown jewel. My tuition was $12,000 a year then, and scholarships obtained from Mr. Mullins's help covered most of it.

My first year was enjoyable. The culinary program touched on nearly all the world's cuisines and their rich culture and heritage, broadening my horizons to include different cultures and races from France, Spain, Iran, Turkiye, Morocco, and other cultures.

As for Black culture, the Black students rolled deep on campus. We had a Black student union, which I joined, and, to my amazement, the historical Divine Nine, Black Sororities, and fraternities. Yes! At a Culinary school.

I didn't know much about fraternities. However, my roommate, Abdullah, a New York brother, encouraged me to pledge Phi Beta Sigma alongside him. It was his dream. I accepted. And why not? Abdullah was a good Muslim brother whom I trusted. We were joined by Moe Solomon, a brother from Newark, New Jersey, who was massive as a moose. Although very intimidating, he was kind-hearted, super pro-Black, and brilliant.

13

From the start, we three got along like three peas in a pod. We became true brothers from another Mother. I could connect to Moe's Pro-Black thinking and his impoverished upbringing in New Jersey and Abdullah's Islamic roots because of mine stemming from reading "Message to the Blackman" by The Honorable Elijah Muhammad and snippets of Farrakhan's speeches laced in Public Enemy's "Terminator X to The Edge of Panic." I also listened to Farrakhan cassette tapes shared with me by Beloff, whose Father was a member of the Nation of Islam. I remember Beloff, and I'd listen to those cassette tapes into the wee hours of the night, dissecting the knowledge and wisdom while counting our money from our drug sales.

YOUUUU KNOWWWW!

First-year students typically weren't allowed to pledge. However, the city chapter of Phi Beta Sigma at Brown University opened a spring line after a solo brother from 1990 would be graduating, and they didn't want the IY chapter to go inactive. We had nine Brothers on the Kiyama line crossed in the spring of 1991. You couldn't tell us anything. You'd hear our loud "BLUE PHI" echoing throughout the tunnels, side streets, and back alleys of Providence, Brown, and J&W campuses. Abdullah and I carried our canes around like our firearms. Yes! Blue and white Sigma canes. Phi Beta Sigma originated stepping with canes. And Abdullah and I were the twirl masters, putting on a step show wherever possible: between classes, during lunch, and at every party. We slid the cane down our arm, twirled while blindfolded, kicked it in the air, and caught it behind our backs. We were smooth with it. We were the new sheriffs in town.

CAREMELLO BABES

I was drawn to Shirl's caramel complexion and Muslim-esque demeanor, compliments of her Islamic Indian-Guyanese parents from Guyana. That's where she was born. Shirl also had Catholic origins, stemming from her adoptive parents, Marge and Leo, two sweet, loving White Irish Italians from New Jersey, who adopted her from Guyana at age six after her biological Mother had died.

Shirl and I had become so romantically bonded that we dubbed the Cadbury Caramello candy bar our candy bar. I was her Chocolate Babes, representing the dark chocolate on the outside, and she was my Caramel Babes, representing the sweet caramel on the inside.

On sunny weekends, we'd spend the afternoon on a blanket at a park with deli sandwiches. In the evenings, we'd indulge in the ambiance of Kabob and Curry, an Indian restaurant on Thayer Street. They made the best chicken Tikka Masala and Biryani rice. We'd gaze into each other's puppy-love eyes while gulping down their melt-in-your-mouth Aloo Paratha. Shirl had a twinkle in her eyes that reminded me of the vast stars in the universe. I could spend all day gazing into them. And I did. We spent every waking minute together. I was enchanted with her. With her was where I belonged.

Proverbs 127:3-5
Behold, children are a heritage from the LORD, the fruit of the
womb a reward, like arrows in the hand of a warrior are the
children of one's youth. Blessed is the man who fills his quiver
with them!

BEAUTIFUL

In May of my third year on campus, Shirl became pregnant. Life was real now. The enchantment was over. The cherub that had shot me with his love arrow flew away smiling and high-fiving the stork overhead that was holding our beautiful bundle in his mouth —Apparently, the cherub and stork worked together.

How were we going to tell our parents? We found courage and just did.

Although supportive, our parents thought we had thrown away our careers. Shirl's adoptive parents were more worried that I was going to leave her barefooted and pregnant. I assumed that was the stigma that the majority of White people held regarding Black men. However, because I grew up without my father, I was determined to be a great Father to our beautiful bundle, Jameel, whom we named after Shirl's brother from Guyana. Jameel is Islamic for beautiful.

During the summer of that year, I proposed to Shirl. And how I did so, I thought, was romantic.

Earlier that day, I bought a cake with the question, "Will You Marry me, my Caramel babes?" written on it in pink icing. I dropped it off at Olive Garden hours before our reservation and explained my plan to the staff. They were all in.

Halfway through our entrée, I left the table and handed the solitaire to the waitress. She neatly placed it on the cake, surrounded by sparkling party candles.

I returned to my seat.

Minutes later, three waitresses arrived at the table with a sparkling cake, clapping with the biggest smiles you had ever seen. They laid the cake down on the table. Shirl was bewildered, thinking it wasn't her birthday until she saw the ring and the writing on the cake. I got on one knee and asked, "Will You Marry me, my Caramel Babes?"

With tear-drenched eyes gazing into mine, she answered, "Yes! My Chocolate Babes."

It was official. We were engaged. The restaurant burst out in applause and congratulations.

Shirl and I ordered coffee with our cake and planned our future.

All Saint's Day

On November 1st, Jameel was born prematurely and with many complications on All Saint's Day. He caught a staph infection in his left hip that traveled through his tiny body, leaving him deaf in one ear and preventing his left leg from growing its average length. He spent his first year in Women & Infants Hospital, undergoing multiple surgeries and blood transfusions. Later in life, he would have a severe disability with his left leg and deafness in his left ear.

Shirl and I rented a studio apartment off campus. Shirl continued her education by taking night classes, and I dropped out and became a stay-at-home dad.

During the year Jameel was in the hospital, we never missed a day visiting him. I could now almost empathize with how Mom felt going back and forth to the hospital for her son Bear. It was a heart-wrenching duty.

However, after a long year, it was pure joy when Jameel was ready to come home. Finally, we had our bundle.

I'd miss many Phi Beta Sigma Fraternity events and Eric's home ball games at Brown. I missed his famous buzzer-beater when he beat the legendary Coach Pete Carrill and the Princeton Tigers and when he torched Grant Hill, Coach K, and the Duke Blue Devils. Our work at Eden Park paid off. I was proud of him. He became a four-year starter, Team MVP, Brown University Athletics Hall of Fame inductee, and NBA prospect.

Eric Blackiston -Brown University

But, for me, it was time to man up and be a father. I didn't have a blueprint, *particularly for a disabled child*. I only had James Evans from Good Times and Minister Farrakhan speeches as role models, —And my desire to be a father since I didn't have one growing up.

CHAPTER 3

Lean on Me like Biscuits

Panned biscuits

- **HOT-LANTA**

Ephesians 5:25
As for husbands, love your wife just like Christ loved the church and gave himself for her.

HOT-LANTA

In 1992, Atlanta would host the 1996 Summer Olympics; hospitality jobs were booming there. It was off to Atlanta for us.

From 1992 to 1996, we were doing well for ourselves. Shirl and I married and became first-time homeowners with assistance from a Georgia first homebuyer program and much-needed assistance from John Beckett Real Estate agency, an agency our college friends Loleta and Kara Beckett's parents owned. Mr. John Beckett's son would become an assistant coach of the World Champion 2023 Denver Nuggets. I remember him spending countless hours in their backyard on their court with his younger brother, covered in sweat and full of NBA hopes and dreams. His dedication and hard work paid off. As did mine.

Coming out of the projects, having a wife, a family, and owning a home at age twenty-one felt good. It gave me a sense of being. My Mom instilled that in me.

Shirl worked as the Front Desk manager at a Hotel, and I worked as a nutrition Manager at Georgia Tech. In 1997, our family grew with the addition of our daughter, Sasha. From the onset, Sasha was a free spirit; she

22

began walking at eight months old and journeyed around the home to keep up with her big brother. I wasn't surprised that traveling would be her life.

The school lunch manager

Shortly after the Olympics, I began working as the School Lunch Manager at an Elementary and Middle Charter school in the affluent White community of Dunwoody. Jameel was enrolled in the elementary school, and Sasha was in the Pre-K program.

Since Shirl spent much of her free time at the school as a volunteer parent, the community and faculty offered her a full-time job as a school nurse; she accepted it without hesitation. As a mother, to be around your babies was priceless. And since Shirl was raised by well-to-do White Irish Italians, fitting in the posh community was a breeze. The Children and I took our cue from her.

Convenience

For the next nine years, from 1998 to 2007, it was convenient and enjoyable to have the entire family at the school; Shirl was the school nurse, I was the School lunch manager, Sasha was growing and advancing, and we could keep an eye on Jameel as he adapted sociably to his disability. Our family had each other's back like biscuits. Let me explain:

Buttermilk biscuits

Whether using a cast iron skillet or a sheet pan, it's best to lay out your biscuits so they are touching side to side. Doing so will cause them to rise to their highest.

Reflecting on this teaches me that during life trials, partners must stand side to side, back-to-back, and shoulder to shoulder like biscuits to rise and stand our tallest. Shirl and I were like biscuits, having each other's backs.

As for spiritual support, I had no beef with Shirl and the children joining a Catholic church, as she did when adopted. Often, I attended service with them. My philosophy was, whether Catholic, Christian, or Muslim, Christ was like self-rising, all-purpose flour; he was all-purpose and self-rising. Besides, the church gave out free donuts and coffee and let out precisely in one hour —unlike Pastor Koonce, who kept us there for four to five hours and then wanted us back for evening service ON A SCHOOL NIGHT! It was hard as hell getting up the following day for school. And forget about Revival Week. SMDH! My grades were effed up!

Biscuits are not touching.

Is it okay if the biscuits aren't touching? Sure. They'll bake just fine, but apart and not as high.

SIMPLE BUTTERMILK BISCUITS

SIMPLE BUTTERMILK BISCUITS
YIELD: 6-8. PREP TIME: 55 MIN. COOK TIME: 10-15 MIN.

INGREDIENTS
2 cups all-purpose flour
1 tablespoon all-purpose flour for dusting
2 tablespoons baking powder
1 tablespoon sugar
1 teaspoon salt
5 TBSP cold, unsalted butter
1 cup buttermilk

DIRECTIONS
1. Preheat oven to 425 F. Sift flour, baking powder, sugar, and salt into a large mixing bowl. Cut butter into the flour. Crumble together using a fork or your hands until the mixture resembles rough crumbs. Add milk and stir until it forms a rough ball.

2. Dust the table with flour, turn the dough onto the surface, and form it into an inch-thick rectangle. Fold it over and gently pat it down again. Repeat. Cover loosely with a kitchen towel and rest for 30 minutes.

3. Gently pat out the dough so the rectangle is 10 inches by 6 inches. Cut dough into biscuits using a floured glass or biscuit cutter. Do not twist the cutter when cutting; this crimps the edges and prevents its rise.

4 Place biscuits on a cookie sheet or in a cast iron skillet and bake until golden brown, approximately 10 to 15 minutes.

CHAPTER 4

All my Eggs in one Basket

- **CONVENIENCE COST**
- **THE WAY THE COOKIE CRUMBLES**

2 Corinthians 4:8
We are hard-pressed on every side but not crushed, per-
plexed, but not in despair.

CONVENIENCE COST

Have you ever wondered why the prices at convenience stores like CVS are high? It's because "convenience" costs. Shirl and I began paying the steep fee for the convenience of having our entire family spend all day together at work.

Having our whole family spend all day together at work and home was initially convenient and enjoyable. However, after nine years, from 1998 to 2007, being a father, employee, and husband at the workplace had become a pressure cooker. Often, our disagreements at home  boiled over into our school workspace for coworkers to witness (I was young then, in my twenties, and still learning myself. I didn't know any better).

One thing is for sure: I quickly learned that regardless of color and age, women take up for each other. Shirl had a

28

solid, organic female support system at work that I envied. My male support system was Mr. Coach Riley, the fifty-year-old White divorcee, and a Bud Light after work with him telling me, "Happy wife, Happy Life." That rule pissed me off! Why wasn't it "Happy spouse, happy house?"

However, I had enough sense not to show my anger at work —an angry Black man wasn't a welcome image in an interracial marriage while at work, in a White, affluent neighborhood, in a female-dominated industry.

Even though Shirl hadn't said anything mean-spirited about me to our co-workers, I assumed she had, and I became distant and withdrawn at work and home.

Fear of my organic self

Most of my agitation at work was self-inflicted. I had shelved my organic Black self to fit into the white, affluent workplace. In trying to belong, I renounced my genetically embedded God-given purpose,

"No one can serve two masters. The person will hate one master and love the other or will follow one master and refuse to follow the other. You cannot serve both God and worldly riches." Matthew 6:24

Matthew 14:23
After he had dismissed the crowds, he went up to the mountain
by himself to pray. When evening came, he was there alone.

THE WAY THE COOKIE CRUMBLES

It was convenient at first when Shirl and our children were at the same school day in and day out; However, after a while, having my marriage and the entire family on full display constantly, I felt vacuumed-sealed, restricted, and pressurized. I needed my space like cookies. Let me explain:

While biscuits require closeness, cookies require space to stay "*well-rounded*" and won't bake into each other's space. The general rule is that cookie dough should be spaced at least 2 inches apart.

If cookies aren't spaced out enough, the cookies will bake and fuse into one giant mess.

No set boundaries

Think about it: if sugar cookies and peanut butter cookies are not spaced out enough, the sugar cookie bakes and fuses into the peanut butter cookie, causing the sugar cookie to become nutty. Likewise, in a relationship, one person can be as sweet as a sugar cookie while the other is nutty. Without the proper growing space, the sweet person will soon become a "little nutty." God forbid a person with a peanut allergy comes into contact with the *seemingly* harmless sugar cookie; the undetected bad traits will be passed on to other friends. Now, we have a whole different dilemma. This wasn't the case with Shirl and me; however, fatherhood, husband, and School Lunch manager had fused into one mass. I hadn't set any boundaries. I felt cramped, and I was no longer well-rounded. Like the unspaced cookies, I lost my unique design, personality, and edge.

Space & boundaries

Shirl, the family, and I needed our personal space to protect our energy and emotional health, grow into ourselves, and not be crowded to the point where we had lost our sense of individuality. Jesus knew this when he went up to the mountain *by himself* to pray (Matthew 14:23). He needed his space and me-time.

Space would have given us autonomy and allowed us to embrace our unique identity and purpose —and become well-rounded.

Established space & boundaries.

CHEWY CHOCOLATE CHIP COOKIE
YIELD: 25 COOKIES
PREP TIME: 10 MINUTES
COOK TIME: 12 MINUTES

INGREDIENTS
1 cup softened unsalted butter (16 TBSP)
1/2 cup granulated sugar
1 cup light brown sugar, tightly packed
2 large eggs at room temperature
2 tsp pure vanilla extract
3 leveled cups of sifted all-purpose flour
1 tsp baking soda
1 tsp salt
2 cups semi-sweet chocolate chips or chunks.

DIRECTIONS
1. Preheat oven to 350° F. Line a baking sheet with parchment paper. Combine butter, brown sugar, and white sugar in a medium bowl. Blend for 5 minutes until light and creamy.
2. Add 2 eggs, one at a time, mixing well and scraping down the bowl. Mix in pure vanilla extract.
3. Sift flour, salt, and baking soda separately.
4. Add the flour mixture to the creamed butter. Fold in chocolate chips.
5. Use the number 20 ice cream scoop (3 TBSP) for large-sized cookies, or scoop out cookie dough by hand and lightly roll it to form a ball. Place onto the lined baking sheet about 2 inches apart.
6. Bake for 12-15 minutes or until the edges turn golden brown. The top should still look a little under-baked. Allow cookies to cool on the baking sheet for 5 minutes before transferring them to a cooling rack.

CHAPTER 5

SISTER NORMA GETS MARRIED

- **ASHLEY JORDAN**

Matthew 19:5-6
For this reason, a man will leave his father and mother and
be united with his wife, and the two will become one flesh. So,
they are no longer two but one flesh.

ASHLEY JORDAN

At forty-five, Mom got married. Yup! It definitely took us Crumb-pickers to be gone before she got married.

Her husband, Joe, was a solid blue-collar working man. He made her happy. But the joy was when Mom gave birth to her baby girl named Ashley Jordan. At last, a baby girl. After five hard-headed boys and many prayers, God finally blessed her with a home, a husband, and a baby girl. Although Ashley was born prematurely and with many complications, she was Mom's bundle of joy. No more boy stuff. She and Ashley could do all the momma & daughter things she wanted: Shopping, make-up, and whatever momma and daughters do. I was happy for her.

> At last, a baby girl; after five hard-headed boys and many prayers, God finally blessed her with a home, a husband, and a baby girl.

36

CHAPTER 6
THE LOST & FOUND

- **TESTICULAR FORTITUDE**

2 Chronicles 7:14
If my people, who are called by my name, will humble them-
selves, pray, seek my face, and turn from their wicked ways,
then I will hear from heaven, and I will forgive their sin and
heal their land.

TESTICULAR FORTITUDE

After years of trying to fit into the primarily White workplace, I had lost myself and became some-one other than myself —An Oreo, some Black peers said. But I was immune to that. I heard this from a few Black peers throughout middle and high school be-cause I was an academic brother. I recall dumbing myself down, trying to fit in with them. When my brother Beloff caught wind of my grades slipping, he blasted me for hanging out with them clowns. I had a future, not them fools. His blasting me got my head back in the game.

It was time to get my head in the game as an adult. My Christian upbringing led me to venture to Creflo Dol-lar's Church and Newbirth under Bishop Eddie Long. However, my spirit was still unsettled. I finally joined the F.O.I at Mosque #15. My childhood exposure to Farra-khan cassette tapes and "Message To The Blackman" made it a natural gravitation.

When joining The Nation of Islam, part of the pro-cess is writing a copy of the Savior's Letter in your hand-writing, asking the Creator for your original name, and memorizing the Actual Facts: a list of actual geographical and scientific facts.

Although my Savior's Letter was accepted the first time I submitted it, I had yet to memorize the Actual Facts and become a registered member. However, while in the process, I soldiered with a few brothers, sold the Final Call newspaper, and carpooled to "Saviors Day 2007" in Detroit. At last, I felt like I had found my organic self—no more Oreo. Painfully, although I had joined the N.O.I. in search of my Black testicular fortitude, to some extent, I joined because of those few Blacks who teased me for *talking* White and not being Black enough.

Courage

In my first draft of "Squash the Beef," I initially deleted the next section out of fear of how readers would perceive me. However, I'm done shelving myself for fear of how others perceive me. That's not *my* problem. I decided to add the following paragraph.

It was all a dream.

Weeks into joining the N.O.I., one night, I had a vision-like dream: I was aboard a Mother Plane, seated in a room facing a towering thirty-foot wall. The wall was imbued with digital computer lights that were computing and flashing. Through a small cut-out window at the top right corner of the wall, I could see The Honorable Elijah Muhammad, the meek Supreme Minister of the Nation of Islam. I sat there formulating a question to ask him when suddenly, telepathically, I heard his voice internally answering me before I could format the sentence. "Damn," I said to myself, "he could read my thoughts before I could format them." I was astonished.

Upon waking up, the dream stayed fixed in my mind for a few days.

Al-Jabbar

Weeks after the vision-like experience, out of nowhere, I heard The Honorable Elijah Muhammad's lucid voice telling me, "You are Jabbarr." I brushed it off. But, weeks later, in the middle of the day, I heard it again from the meek Minister, "You are Jabbarr."

This time, I was shook. The name went deep into my bones as if it were a revelation.

Have you ever heard, "Be careful of what you wish for lest it comes true"? I *did* want to be my own man, and I *did* write the Savior's Letter asking the Savior for my original name. Here it was, Al-Jabbar, one of the ninety-nine attributes of Allah, meaning mighty, compeller, and to console. It's also where the word algebra (Al-Jabra) stems from, which means to fix or repair. And I received it from the Black leader who gave Muhammad Ali and Farrakhan their names.

I teetered between declining it out of fear of thinking I was cuckoo and of alienation from my Caucasian boss and the White affluent community. However, because the dream-like vision and Elijah Muhammad were so captivating, I was *compelled* to accept it. Plus, I was tired of trying to measure up to others. Let me explain:

Measuring up

In cooking, we use measuring cups and spoons to ensure recipe accuracy and consistency. However, when my efforts to measure up to my Caucasian peers (and some Black peers who called me an Oreo) weren't yielding accurate results, I felt inadequate. It was exhausting trying to emulate their character and behavior. I was tired of acting and was out of place. If I accepted *my* name, I would at least get an accurate measure of myself. That was the missing ingredient. Let me explain:

Ingredient

Like an ingredient, every person has a unique profile. How do I know this? Out of all the billions of people, past, present, and future, God has never recycled and reused a set of fingerprints, even twins. This meant that I should stop emulating others because *my* recipe for success was precisely measured out just for me. Let me explain:

Recipe

The word *recipe* is Latin, meaning to receive. So, it was time for me to *receive* my life as God intended.

"For whosoever will save his life shall lose it, and whosoever will lose his life for My sake shall find it." Matthew 16:25.

Can you swim?

After I shared my dream with Shirl and my decision to change my last name, she and her parents cautioned me that White America would frown on me and that it would be difficult for me to advance professionally. I expected Shirl's and her parents' response. However, I wasn't prepared for the reaction from Brother Raheem, an older Black Cultural teacher and community pillar to whom Beloff had introduced me years ago.

I shared my dream with Raheem and how strongly I considered changing my last name. He asked me if I could swim, warning me that I was getting into deep, treacherous water. He was speaking from experience. Many years ago, when he changed his name to Raheem, it wasn't politically correct for Black men to do so. Afterward, he lost his teaching job as a public school teacher.

X

I heard their cautionary tales and decided to take the plunge and legally change my name anyway. I wouldn't take on the traditional X, as did Malcolm X and most other Nation of Islam brothers; the Honorable Elijah Muhammad's vision-like experience was too compelling for me to do so. Also, I never felt like the captains of Temple #15 were my teachers and guides. The Most Honorable Elijah Muhammad was. He gave me my name.

But why change it legally when Farrakhan and Muhammad Ali didn't change their names legally? Because I had no problem asking the streets to address me as Jabbarr, especially the ones calling me an Oreo. However, I thought it was cowardly to ask my Black peers to call me Jabbarr on the street but not ask my Caucasian boss and peers to call me Jabbarr when my government slave name would still be printed on my pay stub and social security card. Legally changing my last name ensured everyone called me by my name. It was time to measure up to myself. It was my Rite of Passage.

Time to swim.

Ironically, in the same manner that I was trying to measure up to my Caucasian peers, I was also trying to measure
up to the F.O.I. brothers, which also left me feeling inadequate. I could never match a seasoned F.O.I.

However, I was now Jabbarr, a name given to me
by The Most Honorable Elijah Muhammad, *their* meek
Supreme Minister. I walked around the Temple with my
shoulders squared and head held high. My head was even
higher at work amongst the Black Oreo name-slingers and
my Caucasian superiors until I was out of a job weeks
later.

CHAPTER 7

RITES OF PASSAGE

- **RITES OF PASSAGE**
- **THREE PHASES OF RITES OF PASSAGE**

"If we were made in His image, then call us by our names. Most intellects don't believe in God, but they fear us just the same."
-Erykah Badu

RITES OF PASSAGE

Suddenly, I was out of work, at home in my tattered sweats, watching my family drive to work and school without me. It pained me to see them pull off without me. I always complained about needing my space, and now I have it.

I still don't know what happened. I have two theories: First, I believed the pressure at work had finally taken its toll on me, leaving me feeling like someone had given me a mickey, pushing my life's reset button, and sending me into a short period of darkness. When I rebooted, I was out of work, at home in tattered sweats. The other theory I came up with recently is that I was entering my Rites of Passage, a spiritual journey to accept myself. In hindsight, I hadn't changed my name; I accepted it, along with the tests and trials that come with it.

THREE PHASES OF THE RITES OF PASSAGE:

First phase: Separation

In the first phase of separation, watching my wife and children drive off to work and school without me was a

46

hurtful separation. Also, cutting away my Government name was a symbol of me separating my former self from my social structure.

Second phase: Reposed (The cave)

The second phase, the reposed phase, was three years of joblessness and isolation. It was challenging to find a job then. Thankfully, I maintained the bills from the early withdrawal of my Teacher's Retirement Plan —money that had dwindled to nothing— and the Unemployment Benefits Extension President Obama signed into law on July 22, 2010, which was up in a few months.

During those three years, it was as if everybody had turned their back on me, including my wife, which was part of the Rites of passage process. I had to withdraw from them and what they worshiped and be left alone in the wilderness, as if taking refuge in a cave, stripped of all external pressures and relearning who I am and who God, the Great I Am, was.

Third phase: Back to life

After three years of one-on-one time with God, it was time to be resurrected into society with my new status. That summer, only able to find work in Delaware, I left my wife and children in Atlanta to work as a camp counselor for Black youths at a Kwanzaa-themed summer program at the historic Mother Africa Church in Wilmington. Baba Jabbarr was the surname that the Kwanzaa youth camp honored me with. It means Father Jabbarr in Swahili.

At the camp, the faculty dressed daily in full African garbs. On any given day, Baba Kamau, the camp patriarch, played African bongos while Mother Jamila, the camp matriarch, played the shekere as the students and I sang enriching African songs. We also practiced the seven Kwanzaa principles. My favorite was Kujichagulia (Self-determination): to define and name ourselves and create and speak for ourselves. I was doing just that, defining and naming myself.

With Godly Black love, the historic Black church welcomed me back home—not home as in Delaware, but home as in returning to my roots and original, organic self. I was back to my roots.

God knew the historic Black Mother Africa Church was perfect for reinserting my new self into society as Jabbarr. To me, it symbolized Christ's resurrection.

While at home, I also visited Mrs. Crisby, the Penny-candy lady I had robbed when I was ten. After forty years, it still haunts me. I made her a Senior who no longer felt safe in her home. I apologized to her. Shame and guilt had ridden my back for too long. She embraced me, cried, and forgave me. I walked out crying and free.

CHAPTER 8

THE LAND OF UZ

- **NO WAYS TIRED**

Job 1:12
The Lord said to Satan, "Very well, then, everything he has is in your power, but on the man himself, do not lay a finger."

NO WAYS TIRED

After Mom gave birth to her beautiful baby girl, she'd have to bury her a few years later due to the many complications. I imagine that after having five boys and finally having gotten your joy, only to bury her was traumatizing, maybe even enough to cuss at God. But she never did.

Shortly after that, she had a nasty divorce, lost her home, and became homeless, living on a friend's couch to a friend's sofa and sometimes in her car. Eventually, she stayed with my brother Moses and his wife for a few years.

Moses was out of prison then, had a great job, and was married. His life was back on track. I was proud of him. However, he mocked and ridiculed Mom because why had God allowed her, a Christian, such misfortunes? Mom kept her faith in God under the strained relationship, knowing nobody told her the road was going to be easy, and she knew that God wouldn't bring her that far to leave her.

After a year of their tense relationship, she settled into an apartment and began taking online classes studying psychology.

CHAPTER 9

FINAL CALL

- **SOLDIERING**

Matthew 25:14-30
His master replied, 'You wicked, lazy servant!

SOLDIERING

After my summer in Delaware, I returned to Atlanta with my wife and children and rejoined the brothers of The Nation of Islam. I recall selling the Final Call Newspaper with the brothers on a busy intersection near the Greenbrier Mall, touting, "FINAL CALL! FINAL CALL"!

After about three hours, I felt disgusted with myself. After selling papers for three hours, I only had eleven crumpled dollars in my pocket to show for it. Also, my Teacher Retirement fund had dwindled to nothing, and unemployment was cut off soon. That's when I heard God's voice asking why I was complaining about the eleven dollars when I had an associate degree in Food and Beverage Management.

It was a rhetorical question. Yet I understood immediately.

Most F.O.I. brothers weren't selling The Final Call for the money; they were soldiering for our people. However, for me, it was both. While selling the Final Call was a good source of income for many, I had a Culinary Arts degree, which I could use to make the money I needed to provide for my family. Still, I had buried my culinary talents like the lazy man in Matthew 25:14-30.

That week, I updated my résumé, filled out applications, and went on job interviews. Within a few days, I found employment as a substitute teacher at my local school district, making $80.00 a day—far more than $11.00 in three hours.

Prescribe your purpose.

Although I hadn't yet memorized the Actual Facts and became a registered member, I felt a strong pull from The Creator to move me on from the Nation. I was no longer where I belonged. I tried to stay; however, His pull was too mighty. And I believed I knew why: Whomever you feel made you a man prescribes your purpose. If you think the Military made you a man, then part of your purpose was to go to war for the armed forces. If you feel the streets made you a man, you'd believe your loyalty was to the streets. However, I know God was making me a man, not an organization; my purpose was from Him. Although thankful for the N.O.I. teachings, I can no longer walk in the shadow of the mighty F.O.I.; I must walk in the light of God, cast my

> Whomever you believe made you a man prescribes your purpose.

own shadow, and evolve into being myself. It was back onto that solitary path of purpose, faith, and belonging.

JABBARR'S BEAN PIE
PREP TIME: 25 MINUTES. COOK TIME: 1 HOUR

INGREDIENTS
10 Inch, Ready Crust Pie Crust, Graham Cracker
2 cups cooked Navy Beans
14-ounce can of whole Milk
1 tablespoon Vanilla Extract
1 tablespoon Butternut extract
2 tablespoons Unbleached Flour
1 stick of Butter
1 teaspoon Nutmeg
1 teaspoon Cinnamon
2 cups Sugar
2 large eggs

DIRECTIONS
Preheat oven to 350 degrees.
In an electric blender, blend all ingredients for about 2 minutes on medium speed until smooth.
Pour mixture into Graham Cracker Pie Crust.
Bake for about one hour until golden brown.
TIP: Cover the pies for 5 minutes after removing them with foil or plastic wrap.

CHAPTER 10

HANGRY STUDENTS

- **EMOTIONAL BEHAVIOR DISORDER**
- **A HUNGRY CHILD CAN NOT LEARN**

Psalm 41:1
Blessed is the one who considers the poor! In the day of trouble, the Lord delivers him.

EMOTIONAL BEHAVIOR DISORDER (EBD)

Returning to full-time work after a three-year hiatus was intimidating. It didn't help that my first assignment was to sub at the Flint River Alternative School, which is designed for students with emotional behavior disorders (EBD). On my first day walking through the doors and witnessing the rowdy, Black EBD students cursing the teachers, this was not where I belonged. I thought about turning around and walking back out the front door. But I was stopped by the Black woman sitting at the front desk. She introduced herself as Pam, the secretary. She saw the deterred look on my face and immediately encouraged me to stay. She insisted that the EBD students needed a strong, Black male role model like me and that I had valuable experience from the historic Black Mother Africa Church and the Nation of Islam that the students needed.

I humbly agreed. Because of Pam, I showed up for the next few months.

The sky-blue walls

The walls of the Alternative classrooms were painted sky blue. I chuckled at that, jokingly thinking a psychiatrist chose that shade because the color was serene and would magically calm down the disorderly students. It didn't work. Not even the Clayton County jail across the highway deterred their unruly behavior.

Don't be a fool.

Strangely, they never beefed with Pam. Her genuine love calmed them down —Not the sky-blue painted walls or the police across the highway. Black students, especially those with emotional behavior disorders, aren't fooled. They sniff out the difference between genuine and fake love. If you were there for a paycheck, they'd smell that on you, and then it would be ongoing beef. This wasn't the case with Pam. It wasn't just a paycheck for her. They felt her real love.

Not only were the EBD students hungry for real love, but I sensed that they were also hungry for food. Chances were school lunch, and breakfast were their only meals. After school, there was nothing to eat at home. That's one reason they were always HANGRY: becoming angry from hunger, something I knew much about. I wore their scars. I was a hangry child nicknamed Hand-me-down. I stole food and took up Culinary arts to eat, even though I wouldn't say I liked cooking.

After sharing stories of my impoverished upbringing with my EBD students, they laughed, and we connected because of the similarities in our upbringings. We could relate to each other. I was from their village, with real-life problems growing up, much like them —So much for that fear that I'd never work again if I changed my name. God had a plan for Jabbarr: Giving back to the Black community.

It takes a village, and I was now an Elder.

My first promotion

Over the summer, the district offered me a School Lunch Manager position at Jonesboro High School, miles away from those sky-blue walls. I accepted it! It would be full-time with health and dental benefits and a Teacher's Retirement plan, which was good since I had emptied it a few years ago.

Goodbye, my EBD students. I accepted the new position at JHS, so my assignment with them was over. It was time to move on.

CHAPTER 11
NO LONGER HANGRY

School Lunch Tray -Square pizza

- ## BACK TO SCHOOL

James 2:15-17
If a brother or sister has nothing to wear and no food for the day, and one of you says to them, "Go in peace, keep warm, and eat well," but you do not give them the necessities of the body, what good is it?

BACK TO SCHOOL

That Fall started a new school year for the JHS students, faculty, and me as their new School Lunch Manager. We were in the hustle and bustle of the first day, and I was excited to be back in my career: managing, cooking, and serving healthy, delicious, nutritious school breakfasts to the students. I'm glad God leaned on me to get busy and use my culinary talents. This money I was now making was far from the eleven crumpled dollars.

While serving the first group of students, I wondered how my EBD students were doing. Were they still beefing with the staff? Were they still Hangry? It wouldn't take long to find out. The school's Principal approached me with a group of newly enrolled students clamoring behind him. He wanted me to serve them. The students were my EBD students. After seeing me, they burst into a cheerful uproar. Let me explain: Over the summer, the school district closed the Alternative school from Flint River and relocated the EBD students to JHS. And there I was, Mr. Jabbarr, their new School Lunch Manager, ready to feed their hungry stomachs. At that moment, I knew that although cooking wasn't my passion, I *was* where I belonged: feeding food-insecure students like myself. Knowing my purpose felt terrific.

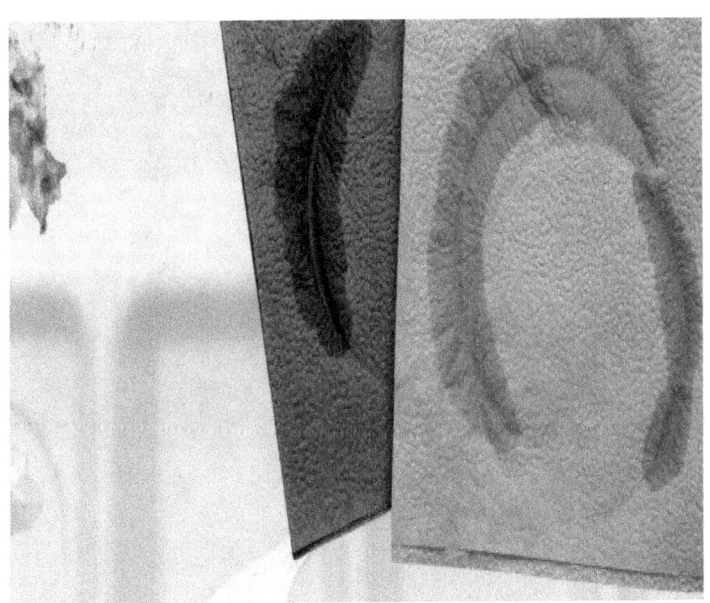

Empty School Tray

CHAPTER 12
THE DIVORCE

- **THE DIVORCE**
- **TAKING STOCK**

Proverbs 4:23
Keep your heart with all diligence, for out of it are the issues
of life.

THE DIVORCE

My marriage with Shirl was over after twenty-two years. It crumbled like a dried-up cake. If I felt like a failure before, now I felt vanquished and shunned.

I wasn't surprised. We attempted couples therapy, but we knew it was done. The therapist just confirmed it. Also, God had warned me that divorce was coming and that I should be prepared to move on.

How did Shirl and I get here? I'm not sure. However, we did at least wait for our children to graduate before divorcing. Jameel was out of the home raising his family, and Sasha was in college, leaving us a cold, empty nest. Everything was cold with Shirl and me: The cup of coffee she made me in the morning, our conversations, our shoulders, and the bed. That will do it: finances and a cold bed.

Haste makes waste.

Honestly, I was thankful it was over. I finally felt the freedom to be myself. Let me explain: First off, I married Shirl in haste. I felt the pressure to marry her after feeling her parents' worrying that I, a Black man, would leave their daughter barefoot and pregnant. To defeat their misconception of Black men not being there for their children, I'd marry Shirl, although, in hindsight, marriage could have waited. Don't misinterpret what I'm saying; my love for my Caramel Babes is strong, but I already had a massive helping of new Fatherhood on my plate, and adding a double heaping of marriage and husbandry was way too much to consume at twenty-one.

Marriage template

Since I was the first of the Crumb-pickers to get married, and there weren't any Black, married men in my life, I didn't have a blueprint for being a husband, so I adopted Shirls' adoptive Dad's blueprint, thus emulating an Italian Caucasian man. In doing so, I, the head of the family, had set the wrong tone for my children by depriving them of seeing their authentic Black nature.

Cubs can't learn to be lions if the father lion is something other than himself (That Oreo). I had to move on from that state, thus visiting World Changers, Newbirth, and finally, joining the Nation of Islam. However, returning to my Christian and Islamic roots was too hard a pivot for Shirl. She was not going to pivot with me. I assumed it was her loyalty to her Caucasian adoptive parents. This left me bitter. Islam was her roots. Our children had her family's Islamic names.

Quiet as a church mouse

I hushed my growl and sucked it up, being quiet as a church mouse. I was afraid to roar like the mighty lion I was because I didn't want to be misconstrued at work as an angry, overbearing Black man in an interracial marriage. I was caged in —think King Kong.

I can't believe I obeyed that stupid saying, "A happy wife, a happy life." It misaligned the order of God, Christ, Man, wife, and children.

"But I would have you know that the head of every man is Christ; and the head of the woman is the man; and the head of Christ is God". 1Coritheans 11:3

Different make and model

Shirl's father was a good man. However, I was tired of trying to measure up to him. His blueprint for being a good husband, Black man, and Father didn't fit me. I was a different make and model. Only God had my schematics for being a Black man, Father, and husband. My son needed to see that. Ultimately, with or without Shirl, I was embarking on my journey.

CHAPTER 13
THE VOID

- **HAPPINESS IS PRICELESS**
- **STD'S**

HAPPINESS IS PRICELESS.

I agreed to give up the house in the divorce. I had no problem with that —until the alimony was calculated at $700.00 monthly. Damn! The high alimony would be financially challenging and leave me little to nothing. I had beef! Yet God told me to pay the amount and prepare to move on. Happiness was priceless.

The Dating Pool.

Shirl and I were no longer close like biscuits. However, we were now like well-spaced-out cookies, having the space to be ourselves. I could now fully embrace who I was —So I believed. The space had left a deep void in me. I assumed taking a dip in the dating pool would fill it. This led me to online dating. In the dating pool, there aren't any lifeguards on duty. It's swim, sink, drown, and swim at your own risk. I've witnessed people drowning emotionally, believing *they* were in an exclusive relationship with someone who was still chest-deep in the pool. How crazy. How can you claim someone *exclusively* while they are still in the pool backstroking? And become emotionally hurt over them? If they're in the pool, you cannot claim them, and they cannot claim you! THEY'RE STILL IN THE POOL!

Online dating pools are separated into serious relationships and casual hookups. Being out of the dating game for twenty-two years, I had no game. I lacked the qualities to be a sincere male friend to women mainly because I was paranoid —Compliments of my dad being murdered. So, serious relationships were out of the question, and I didn't want the emotional baggage that came along with it. I took to the casual hookups. I couldn't drown emotionally in those *shallow* waters.

With casual hook-ups, the women didn't share their real names. They usually used names like Diamond, Paris, Cupcake, or some foreign exotic car. We also didn't share our life goals, hopes, and dreams. It was what it was: a hello, a quick hook-up, and a goodbye.

(STD) Spiritually Transmitted Disease

I wasn't concerned about physical STDs. KRS-ONE had instructed me well with his 1988 hit song, Jimmy. However, I was not prepared for Spiritually Transmitted Diseases (STDs), something my Mom had mentioned.

As my mom explained, a spiritually transmitted disease is when, during intercourse, a harmful spirit that binds you —or the person you're sleeping with— is transferred to you or the partner. Condoms don't protect against this.

Spirit of loneliness

Mom was correct. After my quick visits, the spirit of lone-liness gripped me as soon as I left the motel room, making me feel even more desolate and incredibly lonely again. I believed I would eventually find companionship once I found that one perfect hook-up, so I kept indulging: Maybe Diamond would fill that void. Nope! Maybe Cup-cake. Nope! Maybe Lexus or Persia! Nope! Nope! And Nope! Still empty. This was that part of me that longed to belong, longing for female companionship. It was an end-less cycle. No matter how much I fed it with casual hook-ups, it would never be full. The fast, promiscuous dates were like fast food. Let me explain:

Fast foods

Eggs, toast, and McDonald's cook quickly but get cold quickly. And once cold, it's not worth reheating. Into the trash it goes. The same is true with my quick relationships; they cooked fast but got cold quickly. And once cold, into the garbage, it goes. And, on to the next.

The quick relationships were like a happy meal: There wasn't any nutritional value for my spirit, and they only made me happy for fifteen minutes. Boredom sank in immediately after, leaving my lower appetite grum-bling for the next unhealthy, fast-food relationship. I hated this endless cycle. It wasn't where I belonged.

CHAPTER 14
THE COMEBACK QUEEN

Norma Jazz Wilson's graduation

- **NORMA JAZZ WILSON, M.Ed**
- **TAKEN STOCK**

Surah 13:4 "The Thunder."
And in the earth are tracts side by side, and gardens of vines, and corn, and palm trees growing from one root and distinct roots -they are watered with one water, and We make some of them to excel others in fruit. Surely, there are signs in this for people who understand.

NORMA JAZZ WILSON, M.Ed

My Mom was on point to counsel me on spiritually transmitted diseases, and rightfully so. After returning to college, taking online courses, and studying psychology (at age sixty), she is now Norma Jazz Wilson, M.Ed., practicing as a pre-licensed counselor and psychotherapist. (She must practice pre-licensed for two years, after which she becomes licensed).

The churning

Throughout her life, my mother was churned: Losing her father at an early age, dropping out of Middle school to raise five boys on her own, spending countless days at the hospital with her mother and asthmatic son, and then burying her mother from the effects of cancer. Later, she'd bury her beautiful baby girl, get divorced, become homeless, live out of her car, and be mocked and ridiculed by

72

her son Moses because, as a Christian, why did God allow her such misfortunes? However, God allowed the misfortunes for this purpose: The online college offered competency-based learning, which meant she'd receive full credit for all her experiences and hardships —and there were many! Mom could have beefed with God but accepted where she belonged. She is now counseling others being thrashed by life, including me. And who is better at counseling others than one who has endured that trauma?

Best used by date

Perishable foods are marked with a Best Used or Expiration Date. However, Mom at sixty is a testament that God's purpose for us never expires. However, although God's purpose doesn't have an expiration date, we do, so get busy.

TAKING STOCK

In cooking, taking stock is accessing the inventory so you'll know which items to replenish. As it applies to myself, I often ask myself, what "needs" do I require in my life that I need to replenish? I know when my checking account needs replenishing, but does my faith need replenishing? Ruminating over these questions is what taking stock of oneself is about.

Another reason we take inventory is to find expired food items that should be discarded: Are there things that have expired or no longer satisfy my purpose that I need to dump? Yes! Diamond, Paris, and Cupcakes —Do not think I'm calling my beautiful Black sister's trash. They aren't. They were trying to make do like all of us. It was time to discard my behavior. (The more I catered to my lower desires, the hungrier they became—that appetite I had to discard).

Taking stock also let me notice the good items that I had on hand. I had my Mom's story of overcoming the odds at sixty and my children's stories: Our son had his own family and business despite being disabled, and Sasha, our daughter, was in college and living her best life, with plans to study abroad in Ireland. This I was thankful for. Also, my children understood our divorce. Having a family of his own, Jameel understood the dynamics of a wife and family. Sasha thought her mom and I were out of our minds getting married that young. The thought of having babies and getting married at twenty-one was CRAZY! She shook her head and laughed at us. Who does that? She rhetorically asked. I took that as her forgiving us.

CHAPTER 15

IT'S GRAVY

Beef Gravy

- **SEPARATING**
- **OIL & WATER**

Proverbs 15:18
The Lord is close to the brokenhearted and saves those who are crushed in spirit.

SEPARATING

It's frustrating when your gravy breaks and separates. Likewise, I was devastated when my marriage broke apart after I believed I had worked hard on it. We can agree that marriage isn't gravy. However, it is like making gravy; it will separate if you're not watchful.

With broken gravy, instead of velvety smooth, it separates into an oily mess due to the separation of fat drippings and water. But don't panic; the techniques listed in this chapter on how to fix a broken gravy are effective for repairing broken relationships, relationship techniques I wished I had used during my marriage.

Broken (separated) gravy

Proverbs 15:18
We showed you how to pull your weight when we were with you, so get on with it.

OIL & WATER

It is said that two opposite personalities, like oil and water, don't mix. However, that is precisely what gravy is: two opposing ingredients: Liquid fat drippings and water.

The first trick in preparing the perfect gravy is ensuring that the fat drippings and liquid are measured in equal amounts. If they aren't, your gravy stands a high chance of separating. The same goes for healthy, balanced relationships. If both people put forth the proper effort, they should blend well. However, if one doesn't pull their weight emotionally and financially, the friendship has a high chance of separating, just like gravy.

During my marriage with Shirl, I pulled my weight financially. However, I didn't pull my weight emotionally and sometimes sexually. I was withdrawn and disinterested at times, thinking I needed my space. My one-sidedness was a recipe for a broken relationship. It separated us like broken gravy.

High heat

Nothing will break up a relationship faster than heated arguments. Do not let a heated argument cause you to boil over and run, extinguishing the flame. Relationships require patience, a low constant temperature, and levelheadedness.

A slow, constant simmer

No food will cook if the stove is turned off. Shirl and I were turned off by each other and became cold toward each other. Our marriage had lost its sizzle. We should have found a way to keep the flame burning. *For the record, porn is NOT a good way to reignite the passion— more on this in my next book.*

Keep at it.

To reduce the risk of gravy breaking, stir it continuously with a whisk or a fork; stopping will cause it to separate. With relationships, you must keep at it. Walking away is not an option. Although I didn't physically walk away from my marriage, I did check out emotionally, leaving a one-sided relationship. We failed to keep working on it, we gave up, and like gravy, our marriage separated.

Messy

Unfortunately, sometimes gravy separates no matter how much you work on it. It becomes so oily and messy that it cannot be repaired; it must be trashed and restarted. Likewise, some relationships become so messy that the relationship must get trashed.

As with broken gravy, it's all right to throw away the relationship and start anew again. You are not throwing away the person, just that connection. Many couples separate and then try to rekindle it years later.

Although Shirl and I weren't messy, maybe years down the line, we'll reconcile our differences.

BEEF GRAVY
YIELD: 4 CUPS
PREP TIME: 5 MINUTES
COOK TIME: 5 MINUTES

INGREDIENTS
4 cups Simple Beef Stock
2 or 3 beef bouillon cubes
8 tablespoons unsalted butter
or pan drippings
1/2 cup all-purpose flour
2 teaspoon onion powder
1/2 teaspoon dried thyme
2 teaspoons dried rosemary
Salt and pepper to taste

DIRECTIONS:
Combine Simple Beef Stock or beef broth and beef bouillon cubes in a medium pot and bring to a simmer until the bouillon cubes are dissolved.
Melt the butter in a saucepan over medium heat. Add pan drippings and all dry ingredients and cook for 1 minute. Slowly whisk in the Simple Beef Stock or beef broth and bring to a boil. Reduce to a simmer and continue whisking until smooth and thick, about 1 minute. Add salt and pepper to taste. Serve immediately.

CHAPTER 16

GETTING TO THE MEAT OF IT

Crockpot -slow cooking

- **SANDRA FAYE**
- **THE UNSEEN**
- **IN LOVE WITH MARY JANE**
- **CROCKPOT RELATIONSHIP**

Leviticus 19:36
You shall have just balances.

SANDRA FAYE

After moving on from my divorce; I met Sandra Faye at a managers' meeting. Her strong Faith in God immediately attracted me to her. She was recently widowed, losing her husband to cancer, and was an empty nester. Her two daughters were in their thirties and raising their own families, much like my son, while my daughter was attending college. When Sandra and I first met, she shared her story: A few years ago, she had lost her husband and was reduced to one income, so she was frantically refinancing her home. On top of that, the nutrition department was undergoing a state audit that week. (Every three years, the State randomly picks school cafeterias to audit their books, standardized recipes, menus, sodium fat content, and if we are serving a balanced number of fruits, vegetables, and low-fat milk. The weeklong event is tense).

Although Sandra's school wasn't selected for an audit, she was thrown to the wolves. She was just an employee then; however, the manager whose school was scheduled to be audited quit hours before the auditors arrived, leaving the nutrition coordinator to call Sandra Faye to fill in.

Four days later, after a superb audit, the auditors applauded the Nutrition Department and returned to their state offices. Sandra's coordinator was so impressed with her that she handed Sandra the keys to the kitchen as the new nutrition manager. Sandra's Faith in God had paid off. God answered her prayers; the pay increase was a lifesaver. She wouldn't lose her home.

I love hearing stories of people overcoming complex trials with faith in God. The human spirit overcoming difficulties armed only with faith in God is beautiful. These stories enthrall me. With Sandra, however, I didn't know I would become part of her faith walk, and she was part of mine.

I still had beef with God for commanding me to pay the hefty alimony and leave my home behind. However, after following His command, He didn't fail me. After sharing the story of my divorce decree, Sandra generously opened her home to me. I'd have a place to stay, and I'm pretty handy around the house. Plus, I could provide for and protect her physically and emotionally and help out financially—although it'll be tight with my exorbitant alimony payments. It was a win-win situation.

2 Corinthians 4:18 So we fix our eyes not on what is seen but on what is unseen since what is seen is temporary, but what is unseen is eternal.

THE UNSEEN

After weeks of living with Sandra, God moved on my wallet by leaning on my Director's heart to create and give me a new title with a sizable pay increase. Let me explain: I was promoted to District Chef/Trainer, a newly created position. The fantastic thing is that after the high alimony payment decree was finalized, that's when God moved with my pay increase. When my ex-wife and her attorney devised their plan of high alimony payments, they couldn't milk what didn't exist. They could only milk the pennies I had then (My new position did not exist yet). Alhamdulillah! Knowing I only shared my divorce with my Mom, my director hadn't a clue about it; no one did. That's how I knew it was God. God leaned on her heart.

The king's heart is in the hand of the LORD, as the rivers of water: he turneth it whithersoever he will. Proverbs 21.

The Chef position my director brought into fruition was perfectly timed with the sizable pay increase. I can now afford the high alimony and enjoy a new quality of life with Sandra. That's why God told me to move on.

He had it planned to perfection, and He is the best of planners.

Goodbye, EBD students —Again.

However, with my new promotion, I'd have to say goodbye to my beloved EBD students again. My purpose with them was up. My new purpose was now with Sandra Faye.

IN LOVE WITH MARY JANE

God commanded me to put down the marijuana.

"Yes, God, I'd only indulge in it to meditate."

Again, He commanded me to put it down. I answered, "Yes, God, I'd only use it when friends and family who smoked it come around."

The third time, like thunder booming, He firmly commanded me to PUT IT DOWN!

He had my full attention. I stopped negotiating and did as told. I gave up Mary Jane on the spot that day. He then firmly told me never to leave Sandra —That commandment is still fresh in my mind today. He also told me to marry her —that command I had beef with.

Sandra was eight years older than me. I was forty-four, and she was fifty-two. Plus, I was freshly out of a marriage and wasn't interested in marrying again. I'd follow His command never to leave her and give up Mary Jane, but I wasn't ready to marry again. This decision would later grieve me.

Family Time.

I enjoyed Sandra's family, their gatherings, karaoke, the grandchildren playing board games, and my cooking. Her two girls, Keke and Rita, welcomed me with open arms. We got along incredibly well. They were happy that their mother was happy.

Strangely, Sandra's being a widow psychologically put me at ease—no jealous man was around to plunge a knife into my heart. And despite our age difference, I came to respect her immensely (being younger, I thought I could out-slick talk her and run circles around her. Hell-to-the no!) She *never* let me disrespect her, and I respected her for that. She was the companionship I yearned for: Tough and feminine. I could share my life goals with her as she shared hers with me. This was not a fast-food relationship; this was a crock-pot relationship. Let me explain:

CROCKPOT RELATIONSHIP

Have you ever noticed that when we use a crockpot, we put our food in it and walk away, placing our complete trust and faith in it? We don't monitor it. We trust it. This is how I felt with Sandra: I felt safe putting my all into the relationship, trusting it, and not constantly worrying about her intentions or whereabouts. As a healthy adult, no one wants their whereabouts monitored throughout the day: Where are you? What time are you heading home? Does it take that long?

Knowing what's going on in your partner's daily

life is normal, and the respect of letting your partner know if you will be late or out with the buddies is warranted. However, suspicion without concrete evidence will eat you alive. (Remember, like cookies, people need their space). In the Quran, suspicion, in some cases, is considered a sin that should be avoided.

O You who believe! Eschew much suspicion, for in suspicion in some cases is a sin. And do not spy into the secrets of one another. Surah 49:12 (the Apartments)

Trust is vital for mental health. I trusted Sandra only because I trusted God. I trusted his commandment never to leave her. Like a crock-pot, I put my all into Him, walking away, not worrying about Sandra's or His intentions.

Our authentic self

Just as a crockpot slowly brings out the authentic flavors of food, Sandra's and our crockpot-style relationship allowed our authentic selves to develop and infuse slowly. The wild part is that, unlike fast foods that get cold quickly, Sandra and my slow-cooked crockpot relationship took a while to cool down —The coffee was never cold.

Unlike fast-food-style relationships, our slowly cooked relationship created a long-lasting, genuine friendship full of tender, succulent moments, much healthier than fast-food-style relationships.

CHAPTER 17
THE LIFT

Jameel's medical lift

- TAUNTED & BULLIED
- PRAYERS ANSWERED

1 Peter 5:6
Therefore, humble yourselves under the mighty hand of
God, that He may exalt you at the proper time.

TAUNTED & BULLIED

As mentioned earlier, at birth, my son caught a staph infection that left him disabled. He's deaf in one ear and needs to wear a seven-inch lift on his left shoe due to his leg never growing its full length.

Throughout middle and High school, he was bullied, teased, and taunted. He prayed for his leg to grow and his hearing to be restored, but when neither happened, he questioned God's power and existence. Did God even hear his prayers?

I also recall beefing at God when I knew Jameel couldn't play high school basketball because of his disability. I wanted to be the loudest parent in the stands, yelling, "That's my boy!" But that would never happen. As a father, that sunk me into depression. Did God turn His back on me?

Not a saint

At eighteen and out of high school, Jameel applied for Supplemental Security Income (SSI), which was a waiting game. While waiting, he applied for many jobs. However, due to his disability, jobs were reluctant to hire him. Even McDonald's turned him away. (After the interview, an insider told him the hiring manager didn't want to take a chance on his disability).

With the difficulty in finding a job and SSI backed-logged, Jameel "*borrowed*" an item or two from Walmart, landing him in jail. From age seventeen to twenty-two, this was the fourth time that he was incarcerated, giving him a three-month bid, probation, and a felony record. Since jobs were difficult to find due to disability discrimination, having a felony record almost assured that he wouldn't find work. But God had plans for Jameel.

Standing on business

After Jameel's release and SSI kicking in, he still needed to find work; SSI benefits were helpful but meager, and he wasn't the type to lay around at home while his girl worked at Chuck e Cheese. Only one business gave him an opportunity—a small, independently owned audio CD store located on Tara Blvd. The brother and a good mentor gave Jameel a job burning audio CDs for up-and-coming ATL Artists. However, after a few years of working there, digital music slowly replaced CDs, causing The CD store to close its doors.

Not wanting to rely on SSI, Jameel, being computer savvy, convinced the owner to allow him to rebrand the store into a digital company. Surprisingly, the disabled young man, whom peers teased and businesses shunned, was a bonafide entrepreneur. The business took off!

Months later, I remember when he returned his SSI check back to the state because he no longer needed their assistance.

> **The disabled young man, whom peers teased, and businesses shunned, was a bonafide, entrepreneur.**

Although Jameel couldn't play high school sports, I no longer beef with God; I'm in love with God now. He had a different assignment for JET than dunking a basketball: Being a successful entrepreneur and a social media influencer (@jetismusic) who has touched the lives of tens of thousands of disabled children with his *Dripability and Not Disability* campaign, giving them the courage and self-esteem to live their lives fully. He has also touched the hearts of parents with disabled children, letting them know there is hope for their children. He is where he belongs, on assignment.

PRAYERS ANSWERED

When Jameel prayed for his leg to grow and his hearing to be restored, he questioned God's power and existence. Did God even hear his prayers? Yes, God heard. However, prayers didn't change his disability; They changed him to overcome his disability.

Today, Jameel still gets teased online (Social media is cruel), but their teasing is only because they are jealous of how a disabled young man can become wealthy and have a beautiful wife and child while they, fully abled beings, are still struggling to make ends meet.

> **Prayers do not always change the situation. They changed you for the situation.**

Jameel smiles and shrugs his shoulders, knowing their beef should be with God and not him. You cannot achieve excellence by being envious of others who show their gifts. Those who tease him have gifts, but their envy deprives them of acting on them. Jameel only accepted himself in God, with his flaws, gifts, and disabilities.

Jameel Wilson @jetismusic

CHAPTER 18
BREAKING BREAD

Fresh Baked Bread

- KNEADING HELP
- OVER-KNEADING
- PROOFING
- REST

KNEADING HELP

In baking, kneading is working the dough, *usually by hand*, to develop the glutens in the flour, which gives bread its support and structure. If the dough isn't kneaded, it will lack strength and fail to rise when baked. Reflecting on this, Jeremiah 1:5 reads, *"Before I formed you in the womb, I knew you. Before you were born, I set you apart"*.

That verse nearly sounds like God forming bread, kneading it, and allowing it to rest. However, He's talking about man. Early on, God put His hands on Jameel and began kneading him to develop strength and structure in him.

OVER KNEADING

Can you over-knead the dough? Yes, over-kneading causes it to become overworked and rigid, causing the baked bread to break and crumble easily. The same is valid with needy personalities. Just as the over-kneaded bread will break and crumble easily, needy friends and family members become unhinged emotionally when you decide to stop being their enabler.

But, from the start, Jameel's mother and I decided never to let him become needy or use his disability as an excuse.

Like most teens, he wanted a cell phone when he was young. So, I bought him an outdated, pre-paid phone that resembled more of a black brick. I thought that having a bulky dinosaur of a phone would provoke him to do it for himself. And I was right. Although he loved his artifact, he desired to buy his own phone. I smiled. Mission accomplished.

When he turned twenty, I gave him my old, silver, 1991 Nissan Maxima GLE with 290,000 miles. It puttered, smoked, dripped, reeked of burnt oil inside, coughed, and sounded asthmatic when cranked. Frustrated by the many breakdowns and maintenance, he said, "I can't wait to buy *my* car!"

Exactly! I agree, son. And Social Security Disability Insurance (SSI) payments weren't enough. You'd have to work. And that he did.

The soul of the lazy man desires and has nothing; but the soul of the diligent shall be made rich.
Proverbs 13:4

PROOFING

Proofing is the process in which the dough is set aside and allowed to rest and rise before baking. During this period, yeast produces gases, causing the dough to rise. However, if you add too much yeast, the dough will over-inflate, burst, and collapse. (Adding extra yeast to your dough will not cause it to rise higher. The extra yeast's gas will be released, leaving you with flattened dough).

Learning from this, it is human nature to over-yeast who we are and embellish and exaggerate our worth. That's the same as adding too much yeast to the dough; eventually, your ego will over-inflate, pop, and become deflated when the *"proof"* of who *you* are emerges.

Jameel was never ashamed of who he was, never overembellished himself, and learned to embrace himself with all his disabilities.

Get rid of the old yeast so that you may be a new unleavened batch—as you really are. 1Corithians 5:7

REST

Allowing bread dough to rest at the correct times is a distinct advantage. This allows the gluten to relax, form a superstructure, and achieve lightness.

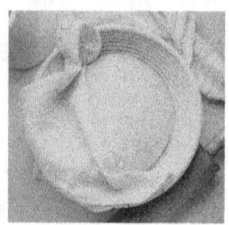

After I started dating Sandra, I asked God: Why the commandment not to leave her? He answered that I needed rest from parenting. (My ex-wife and I were twenty when we had children, and it was exhausting. Yes! Parenting is exhausting). Resting from parenting after my children were grown gave me a sense of lightness, as if a burden was lifted (PTA and teacher meetings).

God even rested after creating the heavens and earth. No, God didn't need to rest; however, He did.

And on the seventh day, God ended His work, which He had done, and He rested *on the seventh day.* Genesis 2:2-3.

Relaxing your mind and spirit after completing a task, divorce, or parenting is okay. Like bread dough, allowing yourself to rest at the correct times provides relaxation and will enable you to achieve lightness. It's part of the proofing (proving) stage, where you find the truth of who you are.

Sandra and I were Empty Nesters, and I needed the rest to focus on myself and Sandra and concentrate on my new position as the Chef/Trainer at the Career Academy.

CHAPTER 19

THE CUSTODIAN: PART 1

- THE CUSTODIAN PART I
- GOD'S WILL

THE CUSTODIAN: PART I

The Career Academy campus is beautiful. It's nestled across from a grassy park where students and faculty can walk, eat, and study. My kitchen was state-of-the-art, and the principal and staff welcomed me warmly, except for the custodian. He was a youthful, tall, and slender white guy with menacing tattoos running the length of his arms.

Strangely, he walked past me when I spoke to him, ignoring me. Whenever I talked to him, I got his cold shoulder and silent treatment. A part of me thought he was racist. Anyway, I thought not to waste my breath talking to him again; I could also give him the cold brush-off. And that I did. (Stay tuned for The Custodian part II).

1 Peter 4:10-11
You should use whatever gift you have received to serve others as faithful stewards of God's grace in its various forms.

GOD'S WILL

Weeks into my new position at The Career Academy, my new Principal asked me to increase our lunch and breakfast meals to accommodate a new group of students enrolling that day. Surprisingly, my EBD students were the new group strolling through my serving line. I can't make this stuff up. The school district moved the EBD students again and relocated them to my newly assigned school at The Career Academy. It was at that moment that I knew my assignment thoroughly. I was to serve food-insecure students, like myself, who were written off for stealing food to eat and who were mocked for their "Hand-me-down" clothes like me. It was full circle for me. It wasn't a job; it was my purpose wrapped inside my career. I was no longer swimming. I was walking on water by faith. *Matthew 14:22-29*

> It was then that I knew my assignment thoroughly. I was to serve food-insecure students who were written off.

Over the next few years, I enjoyed working at the Career Academy. I could rest knowing I was a servant of God for my EBD students. I loved serving and watching them mature, grow, and graduate.

CHAPTER 20
WINE & GEL

Wine & Jell-O

- LET IT BREATHE
- JELL-O

Genesis 2:7
And the LORD God formed man of the dust of the ground, and breathed into his nostrils the breath of life, and man became a living soul.

LET IT BREATHE

After graduating with a degree in English Language and Literature from Georgia College, our daughter Sasha moved to Ireland to continue her education at the University of Limerick. My heart ached to see her move so far away. However, I understood. Sasha was a free spirit who was cooped up with her parents throughout elementary, middle, and high school. Like me wanting my space, I imagine she wanted her space to breathe like fine wine. Let me explain:

THE BENEFITS OF LETTING PEOPLE BREATHE

● Letting wine breathe supports its full potential, allowing it to reflect all it truly is. Likewise, letting people breathe allows their full potential to emerge.

● Letting wine breathe unwinds the tightness, as letting a person breathe will unwind their tightness.

● Breathing opens a young wine to show more complexity and soften the bitterness. Giving Sasha space will ease the harshness and help her embrace her complexity.

• With an older wine, letting it breathe will wake it up from its long slumber and revive its liveliness. Letting an older person have their space can restore their vitality.

Cork & bottle

Vegan Raspberry Jell-O

JELL-O

R elationships are like making Jell-O; it requires timing and a chill environment. If you're adding fruit, the Jell-O must be at a specific gelled state before adding, lest the fruit fall to the mold's bottom (The Jell-O may not *yet* be solid enough to hold the fruit).

Likewise, in a newly forming relationship, it's not a good idea to add your money problems, past relationships, religious philosophy, and mental challenges too early. Like Jell-O, it may not yet be solid enough to withhold that information. I've learned this the hard way. Let me explain:

It didn't sit well.

After two years with Sandra, I divulged my thoughts regarding her daughters, thoughts I wished I had kept to myself. Sandra and my friendship hadn't fully solidified strong enough like Jell-O yet to withhold what I shared. Just like adding fruit too early into Jell-O, what I had shared regarding her girls didn't sit well. Thankfully,

110

Sandra and I continued gelling afterward. However, the backlash was awful. My excellent relationship with her daughters had become unpleasant, and the girls and I had become distant. We still

> **Some things aren't meant to be shared.**

had a family night, but it was different. The daughters and I rarely spoke, and we only kept our peace for Sandra's sake. In hindsight, some things aren't meant to be shared.

Adding fruit too late

While it's not advisable to talk about religion, marriage, and politics before the friendship has completely gelled, specific information, such as having children or being involved with someone, should be disclosed immediately. Not sharing vital information long after the relationship has solidified is wrong! It's withholding the truth, and that's not fair. It's like attempting to add the fruit inside a solid Jell-O long after it is solid; it's too late!

When Sandra and I saw our future gelling together, we shared all the critical information upfront. I just shared too much too early.

Words hurt.

God made words powerful. He used them to create the universe. He said, "Let there be." And it was so.

As words create, some words will destroy *even with the best intentions*. It's like toothpaste. Once it's out of the tube, there is no going back. I strongly caution against uttering hurtful words to your children or mate. The hateful words are forever embedded in their hearts and psyches, *even after you apologize*. And trying to take those words back out of their heart long after they've been sealed is like taking the fruit out of a solid-formed Jell-O without destroying the mold. It's an impossible task. However, professional therapy exists for such reasons: removing ill-willed fruit from a solid-formed heart and mind without destroying the mold.

I uttered some hurtful things to my ex-wife early in our marriage, and some thirty years later, she's still hurt. At that time, I believed that I was getting stuff off of my chest; however, now, what I voiced could have amounted to verbal abuse. May God forgive me.

James 3:4-5 Take ships as an example. Although they are so large and are driven by strong winds, they are steered by a very small rudder wherever the pilot wants to go. Likewise, the tongue is a small part of the body, but it makes great boasts.

I could dish it out, but…

After taking my foot out of my mouth regarding my opinion regarding Sandra's daughters, I sought my brother Moses' advice. He being my brother, I thought he'd offer genuine advice. I was wrong. Imagine seeking help from a loved one, and they rebuke you with an emotional beatdown. I clearly understood what Mom endured when she was staying with him. His fiery words left me wounded. The Bible reads, *"Better is open rebuke than hidden love."* *Proverbs 27:5.* However, I questioned, was this love or beef? Or maybe I couldn't stand the heat in the kitchen and had to get out! This is another reason professional counseling exists: It's confidential; what you share will not be thrown in your face, shared, or used against you.

Since then, I've learned to bite my tongue, be careful of whom I confide in, including my loved ones, and take it up with my therapist and or God!

Salty

The tipping point came a few weeks later when Moses flew into Atlanta for my birthday weekend. When I pulled up to Hartsfield-Jackson International, he was SALTY at the fifteen minutes he waited. Instead of hugs and a brotherly embrace, I was met with shouting.

Although Moses had settled down and was married, something in him changed when he left prison. He had become selfish, constantly beefed, and stayed salty (ironically leaving *us* with high blood pressure, just as having too much  salt would do). And just as too much salt can ruin a meal, too much of Moses destroys our family outings. However, Moses isn't wrong —if used in moderation, like salt.

The boiling point

While at the airport, the boiling point came when he said, "While you had me waiting, I called Shirl, my sister In-Law! She's on her way to pick me up! I'm going to stay with her!"

My heart dropped. He's talking about my ex-wife and my ex-home that I gave up in a painful divorce, that I'm still paying for! N****! HAVE YOU LOST YOUR MIND? I was now SALTY marinating in his detestable words. Let me explain:

Marinating

Marinating is putting meat or vegetables in a mixture of oil, vinegar, wine, and spices before cooking to enhance flavor. Likewise, when you chill and marinate with a person, their habits infuse with yours. If you chill with a positive person, more good qualities are imparted to you. However, the longer you marinate with a negative person, the more you absorb their negative behavior. I was absorbing my big brother's saltiness. But I refused to let him drive my blood pressure up, not on my birthday weekend. I politely pulled over, let him out with his bookbag, and pulled off. Deuces. He can wait for his *"Sister-In-Law."* We parted ways. We haven't spoken since. I would never cater to him again. Let me explain:

Catering

Catering is the professional provision of food and drinks at a social event or other gathering, which can be fun and profitable. However, catering to a relationship can be a headache. Catering excessively to others, even family members, is mentally draining!

I felt obligated to cater to Moses because he was older, and I did so to strengthen our family. It was where I thought I belonged: under his wing. I'd shape my words and behavior to cater to his interests and expectations. However, it seemed that no matter what I did or said, there was no pleasing him. As a teen, I was called Hand-me-down because I wore Moses' hand-me-down clothes, which I happily accepted—no problem. But I didn't have to wear his hand-me-down funky-ass attitude.

As his youngest brother, under his wing, wasn't where I belonged. It was time to stop looking for other people's external validation, including family.

God's mercy

Moses never met Sandra nor stepped foot into our home. And rightfully so. He was a toxic fruit. Let me explain:

Toxic fruits that ruin Jell-O

The instructions on the Jell-O box and agar agar powder recommend not adding fresh pineapple, kiwi, gingerroot, papaya, or guava. Although these fruits are lovely, they contain toxic enzymes that will stop gelatin from gelling (it'll stay Slurpee). These fruits are like toxic people. They appear fresh and healthy on the outside, but their poisonous behavior will stop a friendship from gelling.

God wouldn't allow Moses' toxicity into my new life with Sandra, lest Moses intentionally prevent Sandra and me from gelling. Trust me, some family members and close friends will do that. That's why you should put God first: What God has joined together, let no one separate—Mark 10:9. (God protects His assignments.)

Vegan Fresh Fruit Jell-O

VEGAN FRESH FRUIT JELLO

YIELD: 2 CUPS
COOK TIME: 4 MINUTES
READY IN: 2 HOURS

INGREDIENTS
1 ½ teaspoons Agar Agar Flakes (use ¾ teaspoon if
using Agar Agar Powder)
1 cup 100% Red Grape Juice
1 cup water
¼ cup White Granulated Sugar
8 ounces of fresh raspberries whole (optional)
-You can use any fruit, but avoid fresh pineapple, kiwi,
gingerroot, papaya, or guava.

DIRECTIONS:
Add the agar agar flakes or powder, water, fruit
juice, and sugar to a pot on the stove. Bring to a
boil, stirring regularly, and let boil for 2 minutes.
Pour it out into serving bowls or glasses.
If adding fruit, chill in the refrigerator for about 1 hour
or until it has a thick jelly-like consistency. Add the fruit,
spreading it evenly. Place back in the refrigerator for
about 1 hour to
to set.

CHAPTER 21

TROUGH THE FIRE

- **THROUGH THE FIRE**
- **MISE-EN-PLACE**

1 Peter 4:12
Beloved, do not be surprised at the fiery trial when it comes upon you to test you as though something strange was happening."

THROUGH THE FIRE

The doctor's diagnosis left us numb. Three years into our new life together, Sandra Faye was diagnosed with stage-four bladder cancer. We were floored. As a result, she will lose her bladder, kidney, and maybe even her life.

My only experience with cancer was when it claimed my Grandmother, Barbara Jean, and I saw my Mom wailing buckets of tears. Valium and Jesus were Mom's best friends during that time.

I was seven when it happened and was too young to comprehend the pain and agony that my mother was in. However, today, I understand *somewhat*. Seeing how the effects of cancer and chemo had rapidly aged Sandra, causing her radiant, almond-colored skin to age, darken, and dull rapidly the same way it aged my Grandmom, a youthful, electrifying forty-two-year-old, into a feeble, lifeless body. And although Sandra's alive, I miss her liveliness. I miss her company. I miss our conversations. She went from being full of life to a lifeless shell of her former self. Cancer SUCKS!

Purpose for others

"I wasn't built for this!" I'd beef to God, but He reminded me of His commandment not to leave Sandra. It was my assignment to be there for her.

It was now clear that God's purpose was for the service of others, no matter how uncomfortable it was. As my purpose was to feed my EBD students, my purpose was now to console Sandra through her grief, no matter how uncomfortable it was for me —Ironically, one of the attributes of the name Jabbar is Consoler.

Ephesians 2:10
For we are His workmanship, created in Christ Jesus for
good works, which God prepared beforehand that we should
walk in them.

MISE-EN-PLACE

One of our first lessons in culinary school is mise-en-place, French for "put in place." This means all ingredients are prepped, tools are gathered, and everything is organized before cooking begins.

After I stopped beefing with God, I learned He had already put all I needed to care for Sandra in place. As a chef, I'm skilled at grocery shopping, cooking, cleaning, and laundry (Chefs wash and iron tablecloths and cloth napkins). Having my culinary skills, my courage grew. I can do these chores for Sandra. My faith in God was intact. Being a Caregiver to Sandra would be doable. She is my purpose. She was assigned to me by God. I'm her cut man fighting alongside this female warrior!

CHAPTER 22

TIME & TEMP

- ## TIME & TEMPERATURE ABUSE

Proverbs 15:18
Hot tempers cause arguments, but patience brings peace.

TIME AND TEMPERATURE ABUSE

F ood can be dangerous. It can look cooked but be undercooked on the inside, leading to foodborne illness, hospitalizations, and deaths. The same is true with most of society. Many people appear fine outwardly but could quietly battle depression internally, leading to illness. That was me.

After Sandra's chemo treatments, I'd put on a happy face around other people. However, I was constantly irritable. It irritated me when people called Sandra, wanting to talk for a long time, knowing she was weakened by chemo. Could they not hear in her shallow voice that she was too weak to speak? Yet they continued to yap about their long day. They failed to read the emotional temperature of the room and adequately adjust. I often grabbed the phone and hung up! I know they're calling out of love, but I was furious that they ignored Sandra's inability to talk. I had beef with that!

Listening

Genuine listening is equivalent to a solid hug and embrace. When a person is grieving, just listen without offering advice, criticism, or a damn recipe concoction for cancer-killing! I don't know how many times someone gave us a damn recipe for killing cancer! Beet juice, turmeric, sea moss, this, or that! I understand

> **Genuine listening is equivalent to a solid hug and embrace.**

they mean well; however, we don't have the mental space to discuss cancer-killing concoctions. Our minds are too jammed-packed with apprehensions. But thanks for the love.

Anticipatory grief

After sharing my grief with my mom, she strongly encouraged me to book a session with my therapist immediately! Mom couldn't operate as my therapist and my mom. She did, however, explain to me Anticipatory grief, which is grief or fear before the loss happens.

Although I cannot diagnose myself, I believe I was showing signs of anticipatory grief. It grieved me to imagine life without Sandra. Just thinking about it made me lonely and afraid. My mom was right. I needed my session immediately to re-calibrate. Let me explain:

125

Calibrate

Since the outside appearance of cooked food can be mis-
leading, leading to illness and death, Cooks uses *calibrated* thermometers to ensure food is thoroughly cooked.
An uncalibrated thermometer can misread the internal
temperature of the item, leading to serving undercooked
food that will make someone sick.

Like an uncalibrated thermometer, I was not reading life accurately. I was misreading friends' generosity
and love when offering us cancer-killing recipes.

WHEN TO CALIBRATE

- Generally, a thermometer should be calibrated before every shift: Praying and reading my Quran
  and Bible during dawn calibrated my spirit, attitude, and mindset before the beginning of the day.

- Always calibrate a thermometer that has been
  dropped on the floor: Sandra's cancer floored me,
  leaving me off-balance. This was a pertinent time
  to go into my prayer closet, pray, and re-calibrate.

- As it is a good idea to calibrate a thermometer as
  often as possible, it's a good idea to calibrate or
  pray and center yourself as frequently as possible.
  Re-calibrating often helps to read life more accurately from God's perspective.

- Spending time with a solid friend is a great way to recalibrate.

The good news was that my childhood Brother Beloff and I, whom I hadn't seen in ten years, had planned a trip to Dallas, Texas, to meet up. The sad news is our trip was to say our final goodbye to our childhood brother, Lew Hagler IV, who had just passed away.

After growing up in our impoverished upbringing in the Southbridge projects, Lew, a humble giant, served years in the brutal East Jersey Rahway State Prison. After his release, he, his wife, and his children moved to Texas and joined The Potter's House, ultimately turning his life around. There, he served as a Deacon and in the Hospitality Ministries, providing top-notch hospitality to some of the world's biggest televangelists and ministers.

Witnessing my brother go from serving in prison to serving the Potter's House recalibrated my hope and faith in God—salute to you, Brother Lew Hagler IV. Rest in Paradise.

Although Beloff and I spent most of our time in the rental car, driving from Lew's home to The Potter's House and the repast, our friendship picked up where we had left off. Our time together was good therapy. I was recalibrating. We caught up on everything: his children, mine, and our grandchildren. I asked about Mrs. Crisby. He informed me that she had passed a few years ago. I was both saddened and relieved—relieved that I had apologized.

HOW TO CALIBRATE

- You cannot shout or knock a thermometer into calibration. Likewise, yelling at or knocking someone will not calibrate you or them.

- To calibrate a thermometer, fill a glass with ice water, immerse the thermometer in the water, and Adjust it to 32°F if needed. The key is to place the thermometer in cold water when adjusting. That's putting myself in a chill environment free of anger and hostility. Sometimes, it's prayer, therapy, or hanging out with my brothers.

Still stepping

A week after returning from Dallas, I met up with my LB, Moe Solomon, who had flown into Atlanta. We haven't seen each other in thirty years. He hadn't changed much; he was still big as a moose and hadn't lost his meek demeanor. In college, we developed a strong mutual bond beyond our fraternal brotherhood because of our similar impoverished upbringings.

Like Beloff, Moe and I picked up where we had left off thirty years ago; our friendship rekindled immediately, recalibrating me more. In October, we had planned to go to Rhode Island for our chapter's (IY and AAT) Legacy Anniversary Celebration reunion. I look forward to chilling and recalibrating with my other LBs, whom I haven't seen in 30 years. And yes, it's time to dust off the cane and let the youngins know who the cane master is.

Ice water method for calibrating a food thermometer

CHAPTER 23

THE SHOCK

- **HOSPICE**

HOSPICE

After months of aggressive chemo treatment, Sandra's cancer had metastasized. The doctor offered one more aggressive treatment, which was a fifty-fifty chance. If it worked, awesome! If it didn't work, she was given five months to a year to live.

I urged her to try another chemo-medicine, but she was tapped out. The treatments took a toll on her. She was done. She'd opted for Hospice. My heart sank. I heard of Hospice but wasn't clear precisely on their services. I'd soon learn.

The shock

The tallest and strongest men in Sandra's family stumbled as if they were drunk after seeing Sandra on the couch debilitated. Yet they weren't drunk. It was the shock of seeing her in such an incapacitated state. Many of them quietly left with tears streaming down their eyes.

I wasn't immune from the shock. Mine came when I asked the visiting Hospice nurse to give Sandra medicine to increase her appetite. She was weak, and I wanted to

132

build her strength to fight. The answer was no. Hospice does not prolong life. They only prescribe meds to reduce the pain of a person with a terminal illness approaching the end of life.

Wait! What? The end of life! We can turn this thing around. Right? Let us fight!

Reality had hit me hard. I was in denial. Sandra was terminally ill. Once Hospice was involved, the fight was over. I slumped on the sofa, feeling the stress and anxiety deep in my stomach.

Have you ever placed a hot glass baking dish under cold water to cool off, and it shatters? That's how I felt, broken into tiny pieces. As much as I disagreed, it was her body and her pain. It is now God's call. His will be done. I must come to grips with that.

It's not on the list!

After the Hospice nurse rejected my plea for meds to stimulate Sandra's appetite, she further explained that she couldn't talk with me about Sandra's care. She could only speak with the girls. It was the law. I wasn't on the confidential list. I hadn't a word about Sandra's Hospice care. What? I'm not on the list! I HAD BEEF!

Hospice & the daughter

I explained that I provided care for Sandra throughout the night while the girls slept miles away in the warmth of their homes, and I provided care all day on the weekends. The girls only visited when you, the Hospice nurse, visited for half an Hour! Once you leave, so do they.

After mentioning this, it didn't matter. The nurses were cold and stone-faced. I wasn't on the confidential list. By law, they couldn't respond. I was SALTY! It was unfair!

Sandra's daughter, Rita, beefed back, telling me I could pack up now and leave if I wanted to.

Wow! The audacity. I was the one who took Sandra to all her doctor's appointments. I'm up all night standing post! Furthermore, chances were, Sandra would transition on my watch and not during their meager half-hour visits! That was my biggest fear: that she'd transition in the middle of the night while we were in bed. The thought of waking up to her shell was eerie. God, I wasn't prepared for this. Often, Sandra slept on the sofa, and I slept on the couch across from her, checking on her throughout the night. Sandra refused a hospital bed because it reminded her of her Mother, who had passed from cancer, in the hospital bed parked in the middle of their living room when she was young. She didn't want a repeat of that.

I never got any sleep. I was on watch throughout the night, and many days, I fell cold asleep at my work desk. This is one reason I was a second away from taking Rita up on her offer and bouncing until God reminded me of His commandment: Don't Leave Sandra.

I sank back into the sofa, sullen, waiting for their half-hour visit to be up and for them to leave.

The rapid decline

Although the doctor had given Sandra five months or more to live, her health quickly deteriorated in a few weeks. The Hospice nurses blamed it on cancer, but I believe the high-powered Hospice meds made her drowsy, unable to communicate, wobbly, incoherent, malnourished, and dehydrated.

Throughout the day, Sandra sleeps from the pain meds. When she wakes, she squints in agony. The pain is noticeably unbearable. Since she is incoherent and can no longer speak, her squinting in pain is my cue that she needs more pain meds.

Our only embrace.

Our only embrace is me standing her up to drain her urostomy pouch. I could feel her holding on for dear life, though at times, I'd feel her arms warmly embracing me.

I miss her. I miss her so much.

Regrets

I regret not marrying Sandra when God commanded me to. I was disobedient, and now I am paying for it. I did, however, propose to her months ago before we got the news that her cancer had metastasized. She had accepted. But I'm a day late and a dollar short. May God forgive me.

CHAPTER 24

SUNDAY MOURNING

Sandra Faye March 2, 1965-September 17, 2023

- ## SEPTEMBER 17, 2023

Ezekiel 8:1
1 Then on September 17, during the sixth year of King Jehoi-achin's captivity, while the leaders of Judah were in my home, the Sovereign LORD took hold of me.

SEPTEMBER 17, 2023

The girls arrived Sunday at 10:30 a.m., their usual time.

Usually, I go over how their mom slept throughout the night. (we kept a log) However, *this* morning, God commanded me to skip the routine and the pleasantries with the girls and leave. I kissed Sandra on her forehead and left. I may have been rude to the girls, but I learned to obey God. I went to brunch.

At 12:41 pm, I got a somber phone call from Rita. Mommy was gone. Sandra Faye, my love, had transitioned. It was surreal. I sped home, arriving in five minutes. The family members were already there, sobbing —suggesting I was the last one called. I felt shunned and embarrassed that I was *late*.

Sandra's daughter, Keke, was on the porch, bundled in her cousin's arms, weeping. Rita was inside, on Sandra's side, crying buckets of tears. As I leaned down to kiss Sandra's forehead, I heard God's voice say, "You are on time." The embarrassment of being the last to arrive dissipated. God assured me that I was not *supposed* to be there. He had assigned the girls to be there, by their mother's side, during her transition—not me. And rightfully so. She is Mom to them.

What's crazy is that I thought she'd transition during my watch, but I was worried about nothing. Wow, God's timing, grace, mercy, love for me, and love for the girls to be at their Mom's side.

Love of my life

Erykah Badu played softly in the background. It was Sandra's wish to have her play when she transitioned. Sandra loved Erykah since they looked almost alike. I agreed.

When the Hospice nurse and Chaplin arrived, they collected their meds and tried their best to console the family. It'll be another hour before the hearse takes away Sandra's remains.

Once the hearse arrived, the funeral personnel placed Sandra on the gurney, covering her with a red velvet sheet. The girls embraced each other and walked behind their Mother as she was wheeled out. Keke's husband was behind her for support. I admired him for that. Suddenly, the gurney jammed and wouldn't roll onto the hearse. The funeral personnel pushed to no avail. I jumped into action. (For me, it was no accident that the gurney jammed. I believe it happened for a reason.) I found myself behind the gurney, pushing my baby onto the hearse. I was proud of myself. Just like Keke had her husband behind her, Sandra Faye had her man behind her until the end.

Call Tyrone

After the hearse pulled off and the last of the family members had trickled out, the girls pulled me aside. They wanted to talk. They told me I must leave the premises in four weeks. DAMN!

I'd have to pay $600.00 for the month plus all utilities, but afterward, on October 17, they'd be changing the locks, and I'd need to be out.

I was told to take whatever I needed, but they'd sell the house. Momma wishes, they stated.

The gull of them. I was not even given time to grieve their mom. I felt betrayed and belittled. Yet, I understand. The house was sentimental. I get that. It was their childhood home that their mom and Dad had raised them in. I get it. However, they didn't even give me time to be sad. I had four weeks to find a place. It was time to "Call Tyrone."

CHAPTER 25

THE CUSTODIAN PART II

- **THE CUSTODIAN (PART II)**

Proverbs 16:9
The heart of man plans his way, but the Lord establishes his
steps.

THE CUSTODIAN PART II

The following Monday, I went to work to stay ahead of grief; I had a training class to instruct. I wasn't scheduled to teach that day, but a co-worker asked me months ago to cover her class. She asked if I still wanted to cover it. The answer was a resounding yes. I needed to stay busy.

After the class, the custodian who had given me the cold shoulder for the past two years approached me, offering his condolences. I was shocked, almost offended that he talked to me.

With tears in his eyes, he shook my hand and shared with me that he had lost his fiancé two years ago, which left him shattered to the point that he wanted nothing to do with anybody or speak to anyone.

Wow! My heart sank. He wasn't racist or ignoring me. He was grieving. He was grieving the loss of a fiancé and wanting to be left alone, like me.

He explained how he had honored his fiancé by getting tattoos running the length of his arms. Damn! They weren't menacing tattoos; they were in honor of his fiancé. I felt small. He went on to say how he avoided liquor and had taken up art to avoid going into a black hole, the same black hole I was headed to if I didn't change my attitude. He suggested I avoid drinking as well and find an outlet.

With tears swelling in our eyes, we talked for hours, sharing our stories, our loneliness, our bitterness, the isolation, and our fears. And how, two years later, he was in a much better place with a new girlfriend he loved for being there for him. In short, he assured me, life goes on. It gets better.

God had planned this meeting. Keep in mind that initially, I wasn't supposed to have been there; I agreed to cover that class for a co-worker. The custodian was doing God's work. He was on assignment. We now speak regularly. He's a good Brother. He told me to make sure I don't let Sandra die twice by allowing her memory to fade away. Do something for her birthday or take a trip to Savannah, her favorite vacation place.

Final call part II

Later that day, my Director, who had the vision to create the Chef/Training position, handed me two Final Call newspapers. She said a few F.O.I brothers were selling them, and she thought of me. But I believe there was more to it. Just as God leaned on her heart to create a Chef position, He leaned on her again to give me the Newspapers.

143

I took them as a reminder of how far I had come from those eleven crumpled dollars to a monumental Chef position on faith. Yes, I had a few short weeks to find a place to lay my head, but if God can move me back when then He can do it again. It was time to stand on my faith in God and finish my faith walk. It was my Final Call to get busy again. It was time to buckle up.

Peace

After work, I planned to return to the hotel where I had spent the last two days. However, God had commanded me to go home. Rightfully so. I was homesick.

Amazingly, once at Sandra's home, I was at peace. I thought it would be eerie. But I slept well.

And the peace of God, which transcends all understanding, will guard your hearts and your minds in Christ Jesus.
Philippians 4:7

CHAPTER 26

THE ASSIGNMENT

Purple Queen

- THE ASSIGNMENT
- REDEMPTION

Ephesians 2:10
For we are his workmanship, created in Christ Jesus for good works, which God prepared beforehand, that we should walk in them.

THE ASSIGNMENT

It was 8:00 a.m., and I was sitting in front of my therapist, Dr. B. (I usually refer to Dr. B as Dr. Breakthrough because I always have a spiritual breakthrough during our sessions). This morning was no different. However, during this session, I wept, telling her that Sandra's memorial service was scheduled for 11:00 a.m. today, and the repast was at the house.

I explained that I hadn't had time to grieve; I had to find a place to live. Additionally, I was not part of the memorial planning committee with the girls. I didn't know what to expect, only to show up at 10:30 a.m. wearing their Momma's favorite color, purple.

This was strange because Sandra's Tradescantia Pallida plant, known as the Purple Queen, which I planted for her in the front yard, had bloomed this morning. Typically, the flowers bloom in the summer. However, it was nearing fall, and they were blooming with beautiful purple flowers on the morning of her memorial. I told Dr. B. I believe the plant bloomed in honor of Sandra —Sandra loved that purple Queen plant. It was her namesake.

I then shared with Dr. B. my encounter with the custodian and the jammed gurney and how it all happened as if it were all on assignment from God.

She agreed. Then suddenly, she exclaimed, "The Assignment!" nailing it again with my spiritual breakthrough.

Our purpose in life is a host of *assignments:* Sandra, the custodian, and me with my EBD students. We were on assignments from God. Even the jammed gurney and the Purple Queen blossoming were on their assignment, by God's permission.

If given a chance to speak at Sandra's memorial, I'll discuss "The Assignment."

Sandra's day

I made it home in time to clean the house and help Sandra's sister set up the tables and chairs for the repast.

While getting dressed, I heard God tell me that this was Sandra's day and that I should not make it about myself; that wasn't my assignment —My disobedience to this command would later come back to bite me.

The cold reception

By 10:30 am, I was awkwardly walking into the memorial service. The girls and I met eyes, I spoke, and they gave me the side-eye and the silent treatment. I was on my own. I fell into place with the usher, greeting the guests.

The usher was a volunteer from our School Nutrition Department, someone Sandra and I knew and worked with. She and Sandra's brother and sister felt the coldness from the girls and comforted me when the girls hadn't acknowledged me.

When it was time for the family to walk down the church aisle, the usher and Sandra's brother and sister insisted I move to the front with the girls, who clutched the urn of Sandra's ashes. Sandra's sister embraced my arm, telling me to come on, Brother-in-law. She escorted me down the aisle behind the girls and Grandchildren.

Sandra's siblings always referred to me as Brother-in-law. The girls, on the other hand, after ten years of being there for their mom, this is how I get treated, like a stray dog. It hurt badly. Given the circumstances, I'd have thought our beef would have subsided by now.

The keynote speaker

Pastor Red, Sandra's Pastor, was the keynote speaker. He was firm in giving the guest two minutes to speak. Rita spoke first about how the girls had been there with their mom daily, reading her the many text messages from the well-wishers. She thanked them for her mom. She stayed within her allotted two minutes, as did Sandra's brother and sister when they spoke.

When it was my time, I talked about the custodian, the purple Queen plant blooming, the jammed gurney, and how these things didn't miss their assignment. I could hear the Pastor behind me whispering for me to shut it down. I was well past my two minutes —I was nearing five minutes. But I was on assignment. I felt I was well within my rights, DAMN IT! I was Sandra's man,

I left the podium seven minutes later feeling proud until the Pastor blasted me. And boy, did he blast me.

"JABBARR TALKED TOO MUCH!" He shouted.

The congregation laughed. I was the butt of his jokes. I felt humiliated, belittled, and hurt on top of grieving. And this was coming from the Pastor, who had not once visited Sandra during her bout with cancer. No, not once! I was the one there!

"I" deserved it!

After sitting down and pondering, I realized that I deserved the humiliation. I was disobedient to God when he had explicitly told me this morning that it was Sandra's day and not to make it about me. But there I was, standing on the podium for seven minutes —when I was given only two minutes— making it about me. Me, me, me! And I, I, I! And what "I" was to Sandra. And that was wrong! God was supposed to get all the glory. NOT I.

A high look, and a proud heart, and the plowing of the wicked, is sin. Proverbs 21:4

REDEMPTION

I silently prayed to God for redemption. God told me to continue listening to the Pastor and that God would redeem me. I listened intently, waiting for God's redemption.

Pastor Red continued on me, exclaiming, "Sister Sandra came to me about you! She had lost her husband to cancer and was worried about whether you were a good man!"

Suddenly, he stopped mid-sentence. Something had grabbed his attention. It was God. I could tell. God had spoken to his heart. I'm unsure what God said to him, but Pastor abruptly thanked me, Brother Jabbarr, for a great eulogy. He finished his sermon and closed out in prayer. No one chuckled. God's mercy redeemed me.

The repast

It was a lovely day outside—sunshine, comfortable temperatures in the mid-seventies, and clear skies. It was a massive gathering at Sandra's house.

Sandra's brother and I were outside talking about the girl's deadline for me to move out of the house. I had two weeks left. He felt terrible, but I was good. Although the girls were harsh about it, my assignment was not for the girls or the house but for Sandra, and Sandra was gone—it was time to move on to my next chapter. God won't be blessed until I move on. And He was using the girls to prod me.

Blind is the heart-wreath spray.

Sandra's brother continued talking about how Sandra's assignment was up on earth, but her spirit was still around. I agreed, pointing to the blooming Purple Plant miraculously blossoming this morning. He could not see it because someone had placed a gaudy heart-shaped wreath spray in front of the Purple Plant. At that exact moment, a strong gust of wind viciously blew down the wreath spray, scattering it across the yard and showcasing the beautiful, vibrant Purple Queens in full array. (I'm not making this up. This happened). I knew Sandra's spirit had blown down the gaudy heart-shaped wreath spray, unveiling her Purple Queen in full glory.

The daughter, Rita, knew that as well. Her gaze went from the scattered wreath spray to the Purple Queen plant and back to me. She was noticeably shook.

Yup, I gestured with my eyes; that's the purple plant I spoke of at your Mom's memorial service.

It's not the eyes that are blind, but blind is the heart. If we have kindness, love, and compassion, we can see God's position in everything and everyone. God's assignments were real, and Sandra's spirit was alive, blowing down the gaudy heart-shaped wreath, revealing her Purple Queen plant, the one *her man* planted and spoke of at her memorial service. Sandra had my back. I could feel it.

To God be the glory

Many of Sandra's friends and family offered their condolences to me and thanked me for delivering a great eulogy. I Thanked them but refused to take the glory. God took the wheel on that one. Besides, unbeknownst to them, I still had beef with the Pastor. It was a bitch-ass move telling the entire congregation that my fiancé came to him privately regarding me.

No one knows that after Pastor Red offered his condolences to the girls and left, I was still heated and wanted to express my dissatisfaction with him sharing Sandra's confidential information about me, but God told me to stay seated. I did, but only for a brief second. I went rummaging through the audience, looking for him. He was gone. Thank God. God's mercy prevented me from further humiliating myself.

In hindsight, God's mercy allowed Pastor Red to openly divulge Sandra's private concerns about whether I was a good man. This begged the question: Was Jabbarr an excellent man to Sandra?

Yes, through God's might and power.

In the end, as in the beginning, God gets the glory for the story, not me.

Every way of a man is right in his own eyes: but the LORD *pondereth the hearts. Proverbs 21:2*

SMDH

As the day ended and the family began to clean up, I told the gathering I'd clean up, and they could leave. I needed the quiet time.

The last to leave was Rita. She informed me that she had left Sandra's ashes on the mantle.

WHAT! WHY? Why not take them with you? I asked myself.

Looking at the mantle, there they were—a sealed blue box of ashes. Shaking my damn head, Sandra, babe, it's me and you till the end, or until the locks are changed.

CHAPTER 27

THE PURPOSE

- GET GONE
- THE PURPOSE OF OTHERS

Matthew 6:34
Therefore, do not worry about tomorrow, for tomorrow will worry about itself. Each day has enough trouble of its own.

GET GONE

It was October 1st, two weeks after Sandra's death and two weeks before they changed the locks. I told the girls I'd pay half the month's rent since the locks would be changed mid-month. However, they had beef. They wanted the entire enchilada. How Crazy!

I attempted to reconcile our difference by offering the $600 for the two weeks, and I'd take the bedroom and outdoor furniture that Sandra and I went half on.

The answer was no. There wasn't any proof that we went half, which was bull! They knew their mom, and I always split everything down the middle. Besides, I had credit card statements as proof.

Even after having evidence, the negotiations shifted to them needing to inventory the items in the house. I was becoming agitated. But I understood. There was still beef between us.

I mentioned the new a/c unit, the new air handler, and the new roof and gutters that increased the home's value if they sold, which I didn't want to get a dime from. All I wanted was the bedroom and outdoor furniture.

However, God reminded me that my assignment was to leave. Not negotiate anything or furniture. Leave. He wouldn't bless me until I did.

THE PURPOSE OF OTHERS

It was now even more apparent that my purpose was not for me —God's purpose is for the service of others that *He* assigned you to, no matter how uncomfortable. My purpose for Sandra was done no matter how painful it was. My next assignment was to move on, no matter how sad I was. God had already made the arrangements. I just had to walk in them.

Hold on tight!

I hung up with the girls and called my bank for a home loan. They denied me after a hard credit inquiry showed an outstanding payment from the home with my ex-wife. I was furious! That home should have been paid in full.

I texted Shirl. She quickly put my anger to rest. She had texted me a copy of the certificate from the Realhome mortgage company that read PAID-IN-FULL. The light went on for me. Why dispute the charges with the credit bureau and then call back my banking institution when I could ask the Realhome mortgage company for another loan? They had my information, and we had a great relationship. I called Realhome Mortgage, and I was approved within a few hours. God was moving fast. I had to keep up.

Jameel's father-in-law was going through a situation like mine. His wife had died from cancer a year ago, and her disgruntled children were lobbying for the house. He had moved into another home while waiting for the courts to decide. He had given me his realtor's information. She was sending me leads within the hour.

God made arrangements.

Shortly after, I called my long-time friend Pam Patricia, the Secretary from the Alternative school. She had encouraged me to stay at the Alternative school when the EBD students were cussing out the staff, and I was ready to bounce.

We hadn't spoken in fourteen years. She had moved on from the Alternative School and was employed with another School district. The last time we chatted, she was renting a room to a tenant.

I explained my situation. Great news! The tenant had moved out a few months ago. The fully furnished bedroom with T.V., cable, and an adjoining personal bathroom was available for me to rent.

In two days, I packed my clothes, left everything behind, including furniture, and moved that Saturday evening. Deuces!

"God-made" arrangements

God will send you the person and provisions you need for that portion of the journey. Pam Patricia was that person as she was fourteen years ago with our EBD students. Sandra was God-sent during my divorce; my director, with the unseen job promotions, was God-sent, as was Beloff's N.O.I. influence on me at a young age, to Mr. Mullins, my high school teacher, sending me to college. God will send you the person and provisions you need for that portion of the journey.

It was time to pull up the anchor, have faith, and set sail again. It's time to see what I, the student, have learned. I had enough proof to trust God.

CHAPTER 28

THE WORK

- THE WORK

James 2:17
Faith without works is dead.

THE WORK

On Saturday morning, I had a session with Dr. B. During our last session, we broke through with "The Assignment." However, during this session, Dr. B helped me break through on what an assignment is. An assignment is work. It is a task or duty assigned to someone.

Throughout this book, I've used the term *assignment*, not fully understanding that an assignment is a duty from God. Whether it was the assignment to change my name, leave the N.O.I, give up my first house in a divorce, never to leave Sandra, faith without "works" *or being dutiful* is dead. It wasn't enough to believe in God—the devil also believes in God (*James 2:17-19*). I had to do the assignments (work). The same is written in the Quaran:

Your striving is surely for diverse ends. Then, as for him who gives and keeps his duty and accepts what is good, we facilitate for him the way to ease. And as for him who is miserly and considers himself self-sufficient and rejects what is good, we facilitate for him distress. And his wealth will not avail him when he perishes—Surah 92:4-11 (The Night).

Love ain't chocolates.

If it were up to me, my love for Sandra would have been flowers, cards, sex, and romance. But when death slowly walks toward you, love is more than chocolates or jewelry. To love Sandra unconditionally, I had to surrender to God unconditionally. Don't let that go over your head.

That void again.

In the chapter, Taking Stock, I was empty and hangry because I couldn't fill that loneliness in me no matter how much I fed it with fast-food relationships. Now, with Sandra gone, that void came back, which testified that Sandra had filled that void. I now knew that fast-food relationships could not fill that loneliness. Only a God-sent friend will. Sandra Faye was that God-sent friend.

Grieve-itate.

After Sandra's Death, God reprimanded me, telling me that faithfulness to Him doesn't require companionship. He then warned me not to return to my promiscuous behavior. He termed it grieve-itate, a combination of the words Grieve and Gravitate, meaning not to allow my *grief* to cause me to *gravitate* back to that behavior. I obliged.

163

Anyone will do.

During my subsequent counseling session, Dr. B echoed God by stating, "When you don't feel like you are all the way put together, anyone will do."

How right she was. Before I met Sandra, I didn't feel all the way put together, so anyone or anything would do. It was time to "fight" that behavior. Fight! Fight! Fight!

It may be that you hate something when it is good for you, and it may be that you love something when it is bad for you. God knows, and you do not know. Fighting is prescribed to you, even though you do not like it.
- Surah 2:216 The Cow

A good friend

If you have a good spouse or friend, it's only because God gave them to you. Without Him, no relationship would thrive. God must become first in your life. He is The Creator of all personalities and attributes; He knows how, when, and whom to pair you with to bring out your best parts. A God-ordained friendship trumps sex and romance. When the candle flickers out, friendship stays shining bright.

CHAPTER 29

LIFE REPEATS ITSELF

- EXPECTATIONS
- FULL CIRCLE
- CROSS-CONTAMINATION

Expectation is the Mother of disappointment.

EXPECTATIONS

Searching for a home is exhausting. I spent days and lots of gas driving from property to property. Most homes looked nice online but horrible in person. I was disappointed. I called my childhood brother Eric Blackiston, JD (After an injury derailed his NBA dreams, he became the co-founder and CEO of The Mortgage Corporation from 1998 to 2008).

Eric advised me not to focus on the cosmetics: soiled carpeting, holes and dings in the walls, badly needing spackle and fresh coats of paint, hanging cabinet doors, missing floor tiles, and a cluttered backyard. These were minor weekend projects that could negotiate the price down. Instead, he suggested worrying about the silent wallet-killers: the roof, the foundation, the plumbing, the electric, the heating and air, and the air handler unit. These were significant problems that could sink a budget.

The most valuable wisdom he gave me was to stop chasing the home. When you chase anything, it naturally runs away from you: A dog chasing a cat or its tail, a cat chasing a mouse, or an overzealous man desperately pursuing a date with a woman.

166

He suggested I relax and take my time, and the right home would find me.

But how do I make myself attractive to attract the house to me? He laughed and said, "Stop chasing it."

> **My expectations were causing me unnecessary tension.**

Eric confirmed what The Creator had said to me during my morning prayer: to step back from searching for homes, stop chasing it, and wait until December; my expectations were causing me unnecessary tension.

A house is not a home.

Another reason why God told me to take a break from home searching is because when I toured the perfect home during an open house, I felt deeply lonely. Sandra wasn't there to share in the excitement. As Luther Vandross sang, "A house is not a home when there's no one there to hold you tight."

Without Sandra, the place would be cold. I wasn't ready to be by myself. Not yet. I'll listen to God and step back from house searching. I'll patiently wait until December, as instructed.

The Cave 18:16
And when you withdraw from them and what they worship,
save God, take refuge in the cave, your Lord will spread forth
for you a profitable course in your affair.

FULL CIRCLE

My life was repeating itself. It had come full circle. It was as if I was going through my rites of Passage *again*. Fourteen years ago, Pam Patricia was there when I entered the work world from a three-year hiatus; today, she's renting me a room.

When life repeats itself, we believe there's something we haven't learned and thus must repeat it. That was untrue to me. My truth is that the second time around, I fully understood that all my strength came from God. As for my rites of passage seemingly repeating, we are continuously reborn and made new multiple times, just like trees and perennials during their season.

Reposed Again (The cave again)

While I settled in my rented room, God told me my work with Sandra was complete. And He had reposed me in that room so that I could rest. Being a Caregiver was mentally exhausting. Also, my emotional and spiritual compass was in a tailspin. I needed the rest like the resting of bread dough.

Taking Stock (Again)

Resting gave me the time to take stock of my life *again*. I was grateful I landed on Pam Patricia's property, like in Monopoly, and not a stranger's property or jail.

From scratch

During this second go-around, God gave me a clean slate before my next assignment —A clean slate sounds awesome because past mistakes and sins are erased. However, a clean slate means starting from scratch. Everything *I thought* was important to me (my spouse, fiancé, friends, family members, jobs, and even homes) was taken away, and I started over from scratch, like breadmaking. And being reposed in my room was the perfect space for God to knead me like dough, developing my strength and structure, and shaping me into the person He wanted me to be. Additionally, I had the space I needed, like cookies to spread out.

Tested

Starting from scratch tested my faith, resilience, and patience. This was when I needed to lean on God like scratch-made buttermilk biscuits to rise to my highest yield.

"My brethren, count it all joy when you fall into various trials, knowing that the testing of your faith produces patience. But let patience have its perfect work, that you may be perfect and complete, lacking nothing." James 1:2-4

CROSS-CONTAMINATION

Cross-contamination is another reason why God reposed me and started me over from scratch. Let me explain:

In the movies, during a biohazard crisis, a contaminated person must enter a sealed room where they are showered, cleaned, sanitized, and sometimes put in a hazmat suit to avoid cross-contamination. They aren't allowed to proceed into the safe zone until they are entirely free of contaminants, lest they contaminate the area and the people in the next room.

God, having me reposed was like that. He wouldn't allow me to enter the next chapter of my life until He sealed me off and cleaned and sanitized my mind, thoughts, spirit, and heart from all the contaminants of bitterness and anger (particularly the bitterness from dealing with the girls). God would not let me infect the new people, the new space, in the next chapter of my life. This is like Cross-contamination in cooking. Let me explain:

CROSS-CONTAMINATION

The process in food service in which harmful bacteria or microorganisms are transferred from one food or object to another is cross-contamination. Some examples are:

- Touching raw meats without gloves and handling vegetables without washing your hands is a no-no! Life is the same: We must wash our hands (*of some people and habits*) before moving on to the next task or assignment, lest we bring harmful energy.

- Using *the same* knife and cutting board to cut poultry and chop vegetables without washing and sanitizing them between the tasks is a no-no. You should wash, rinse, sanitize, and air-dry utensils between tasks. The same is valid for relationships. I shouldn't take Sandra into my next relationship, no matter how much I loved her; that's unfair to the next person.

My heart, mind, and spirit should be thoroughly cleaned and sanitized before proceeding.

CHAPTER 30

BETTER IN THYME

- SASHA WAS HOME
- OVERWHELMING JOY

Proverbs 3:27
Do not withhold good from those to whom it is due
when it is in your power to act.

SASHA WAS HOME

Sasha, my daughter, moved back home from Ireland. I'm anxious to see her, but I'll continue giving her space. Hopefully, she'll be ready to catch up after I fly back from Rhode Island.

I'm flying out to see my Fraternity Brothers for our thirtieth Legacy Anniversary Celebration Reunion. I look forward to rekindling genuine, long-term friendships and, after *"Calling Tyrone,"* finally getting that *"Window Seat"* that Erykah Badu sang about.

I'm also looking forward to recalibrating and hearing the Honorable Brother Chris V. Rey JD, the International President of Phi Beta Sigma Fraternity, Incorporated, speak as our keynote speaker. I'm staying away from that task.

Culture for service

In addition to our fellowshipping, gripping, strolling, stepping, and chanting, the reunion included community service at the local Rescue Mission, handing out clothes and bottled water to the local people experiencing hardships.

Afterward, we held a Men's Mental Health circle with the community, which I needed.

My Line Brother Sean "Milk" Shivers shared his life-changing story first: A year ago, he went through a double lung transplant after being diagnosed with a severe pulmonary fibrosis lung condition. The lung transplant saved his life. This was why brothers Reggie Lawrence, Aaron Tucker, Toney Harewood, Ed, and Derek Bowmer planned the thirtieth legacy reunion. It was time to celebrate brotherhood and Life.

Get back in the fight!

As other brothers shared their woes, Brother Moe Solomon became agitated. Something was biting at him. He was unsettled at our pity party. He chose to speak last.

Brother Moe closed the meeting by saying we all have similar stories of hardship and pain, but let's stop pitying ourselves. It's time to get back into the fight. He shared Mike Tyson's quote, "Everyone has a plan until they get punched in the mouth." So true. Life had punched us all in the mouth, but it was time we got back to the fight.

He then shared Marvelous Marvin Hagler's quote; "A champion shows who he is by what he does when he's tested. When a person gets up and says, 'I can still do it,' he's a champion".

The men in the circle smiled in agreement. Moe closed the meeting by saying that when an athlete runs through the tunnel, the fans can cheer for or against him. Whether cheering for you or booing, let the cheers motivate you to keep going. Don't lay about in failure. Get back up! Get back in the fight of life.

Brother Moe Solomon left the circle with applause from the Sigmas and the men from the Mission. He was on assignment. We were motivated to get back into the battle of life! It was time to stop playing the victim.

Stop playing the victim.

In this book, during my grieving process, I played the victim and made the girls out to be monsters. I was unsoundly wrong. Grief distorted my perception. I read the situation wrong, like an uncalibrated thermometer.

After recalibrating with sincere prayer, God allowed me to read the situation accurately: The girls had lost their Mom, their Queen jewel, whose value equaled almost the same value as God. Their whole world was turned upside down, just like my Mom's when she lost her Mom to cancer. They could no longer call, talk to, or see their mom ever again, which is another level of grief and hurt. Hurt upon hurt. I wasn't the victim; they were. I lost a home and a friend, but they lost their Mom.

Slow to speak.

That said, I apologize for my beef and hope the girls will forgive me for my negative portrayal. I was hurt and selfish. I should have been *quick to listen, slow to speak, and slow to become angry because human anger does not produce the righteousness that God desires." James 1:19-20*

Forgiveness

I forgive the girls and pray that they forgive me. I cannot move on with my purpose without first unconditionally forgiving them and forgiving myself. With that said, I forgive myself for not marrying Sandra and giving her my last name; that guilt and shame held me in bondage for too long.

Guilt & shame.

Guilt and shame are potent shackles that hinder progress. However, knowing that God is a forgiven God tells me that forgiveness is the key to unshackling myself from guilt and shame. I was unshackled from my guilt and shame of robbing the Penny-candy lady once she forgave me. Also, when Adam ate the forbidden fruit, guilt and shame gripped him; thus, he hid from his Creator.

However, God forgave him and gave him a new slate. Only forgiveness overcomes guilt and shame. (To a degree, I guess Jesus dying for our sins was him unshackling us from guilt and shame).

Squash the beef.

It was time to tear off that self-defeating label of victim and return to the fight of life. It was time to squash the beef with God, Moses, myself, the girls, and the Pastor —It was my poor choice to speak for seven minutes.

It's time to forgive, let go of guilt and shame, and move on with my journey, purpose, and subsequent assignments.

Mathew 25:23
Enter the joy of your lord.

OVERWHELMING JOY

On the closing day of our reunion, the brothers and I stood in the courtyard that crisp, sunny Sunday morning, preparing to sing our hymn. I stood in awe of the sheer majesty of the revamped campus. Johnson & Wales had grown mightily since I was last there in 1992. Sprawling grass fields occupied half the campus, new buildings were erected, and new monuments were built. It was majestic; it no longer stood in the shadow of Brown University but nearly eclipsed Brown.

Then God spoke to me. He said He wanted me to see the magnificence of the campus: The Food & Beverage Management associate degree I earned in 1991 had increased in value. Then, the tuition was $12,000. Now, tuition and housing are $59,000 yearly. What little God trusted me with then had grown into greatness.

Reflecting on this, my body tingled like something had descended upon me. I couldn't explain the feeling until God had me take a trip down memory lane.

If you recall, in 2006, I buried my degree, opting to sell The Final Call, earning $11.00. (No disrespect to the Mighty F.O.I.) He caused me to unbury my degree and talents and utilize them, a degree that grew tremendously in value. I could now describe that tingling in my body as the joy of The Lord:

"Well done, good and faithful servant; you have been faithful over a few things; I will make you ruler over many things. Enter the joy of your lord. Matthew 25:21.

I had entered the joy of my Lord. Thank you, Saviour.

Long ago, God had poured into me, *like a crock-pot,* a talent, trusting me and walking away.

I diligently used my abilities to serve the EBD students, other food-insecure students, and Sandra.

My question is: Can God pour into you like a crock-pot and walk away knowing you'd be diligent?

Better with thyme

The reunion was like Mom's leftover spaghetti: The brotherhood formed over thirty years ago, including my brotherhood with my childhood brothers Eric and Beloff, had developed and gotten  better over time. Like Mom's leftover spaghetti, the Sigma boys from thirty years ago had become balanced and well-seasoned men of Phi Beta Sigma Fraternity, Inc.

CHAPTER 31

IT WILL NOT TARRY

- TARRIED

- GOD'S SIDE-EYE

- GOD BLESS THE CHILD

- GENTRIFIED

Habakkuk 2:3
For the vision is yet for an appointed time; But at the end, it will speak, and it will not lie. Though it tarries, wait for it because it will surely come; it will not tarry.

TARRIED

Returning home after a beautiful week of Sigma brotherhood, I sat in my room, agitated about returning to the small space. Out of nowhere, God asked: How long had I tarried in my room? I begrudgingly answered: A week.

He had me look at the calendar. Wow. I was no longer agitated. I was baffled. It was November 8th. I had tarried for an entire month. I left Sandra's home on October 1st, and the October 17th deadline to vacate the house had come and gone. I was unbothered and hadn't missed a beat. God had me.

Philippians 4:6
Do not be anxious about anything, but in every situation, by prayer and petition, with thanksgiving, present your requests to God.

<u>GOD'S SIDE-EYE</u>

In early November, God commanded me to stop searching for a home because it was causing me unnecessary stress. However, while driving to Walmart, I noticed the small tan house. It caught my attention. It was located down the street from Pam. I pulled over and checked on it, going against God's command to wait till December. I could feel God giving me the side-eye like James Evans from Good Times for being disobedient and looking for a home after he'd commanded me to stop searching, but the move-in ready home was laid back and offered plenty of privacy.

The house was under contract.

Damn! I'll wait until December as God commanded, I sheepishly uttered to myself, knowing His side-eye was still on my back.

December

Driving past the tan house again, some thirty days later, I noticed the for-sale sign still planted in the yard. I wasn't being disobedient checking on it this time; it was December.

The house was no longer under contract. The listing was now Active, with a $1000 decrease. I contacted my realtor to make an offer. After some wrangling, the Homeowner accepted our offer a few weeks later. The closing date was set for January 12th.

I recall Eric telling me about chasing your blessings. The more you chased them, the more they ran from you. This was even true with your shadow (depending on the sun's position). Your shadow will run from you if you chase it. However, if you "be still," your shadow will eventually find its way to you. And the home found its way to me just as God intended: down the street from Pam, which had me thinking. Did God lead me to Pam to lead me to the home? Was that part of His plan?

Sucker-punched in the gut.

The price was within my approved FHA loan —until the Mortgage Lender estimated the additional closing cost at fourteen thousand dollars. HUH?! An additional

$14,000.00! I was floored. I was about to tap out. But God started working. The Homeowner agreed to give me five thousand dollars in closing costs. Cool. That leaves me to pay $9000.00 and 3.5% of my FHA loan for closing.

Since Shirl and I purchased our home using the Georgia Dream Homeownership program. I asked my loan officer about it. He couldn't because he wasn't licensed to do so in Georgia. WAIT! WHAT! And now you are just telling me this? I was furious! But God wasn't. The loan officer forwarded me to another Realhome Mortgage Loan officer in Georgia. The new loan officer called me the next day, changed my FHA loan to a conventional one, and offered me an additional five thousand dollars for closing costs, and I only had to pay 1% of the loan. Look at God.

In addition, my school district gave employees a $1000.00 bonus for the "*December*" holidays. (That's why God ordered me to wait till December) That left me needing $3000.00 for closing, but God wasn't through yet. After inspecting the home, the Homeowner agreed to an additional $1600.00 in closing costs for minor DIY repair projects, bringing closing costs down to fourteen hundred dollars. But here came God with the victory. That morning, a televised news brief showed Governor Kemp announcing that all Georgia teachers and workers would receive a $1000.00 December Holiday bonus and a 5% pay bump. God said to wait until December, and His word is the truth. Closing Costs were covered—and then some!

185

"Mama may have, Papa may have. But God bless the child that's got his own, that's got his own."

-Billie Holiday

GOD BLESS THE CHILD

Outside, I can see the bare trees in *my* backyard swaying from the brutally cold wind shear. It's a cold winter morning in Hampton, Georgia, but it doesn't bother me; I'm in the warmth of *my* new home, bundled in *my* cozy bed, sipping my freshly brewed hot cup of coffee and typing away. I closed a few days ago, said my goodbyes to Pam, thanked her graciously, and moved into my home the day I closed.

The move-in-ready, newly renovated two-car garage, three-bedroom, two-bath ranch with a patio has new granite countertops, interior paint, new carpet, a new HVAC system, contemporary lighting, luxury vinyl flooring, and a jacuzzi. Yes, I lost some things, but I will no longer grieve over them. The home I gave up in my divorce to Shirl is restored. Also, the furniture that Sandra and I went half on that I wanted, yet God said to leave; he restored it. Let me explain: The delivery guy who delivered my kitchen table yesterday had on his truck a well-kept, solid wood, five-piece, queen sleigh bedroom set worth $2000.00 that he gave me for $50.00. I'm not making this up. He said he picked it up this morning after delivering new furniture to a client and taking her gently used five-piece set. He said he needed the truck space for another job later that day. Okay. Thank you, God, for allowing me to help this brother out. And for delivering on your promise to replenish what I had lost.

God has apprised you of this, that you may neither grieve over that good which is lost to you, nor exult because of that which He has granted you.
-Surah 57:23 "The Iron."

Believing is seeing.

In this world, seeing is believing, but with God, believing is seeing. A few weeks later, I doubted a huge blessing from God after He directed my path to Ashley's Furniture.

While looking for living room furniture, I noticed an 8-piece, brand-new living room set on clearance for $1000.00: A chocolate-colored reclining sofa and reclining loveseat, a coffee table and its matching end tables, two matching lamps, and an 8X10 large area rug underneath it. All you needed to complete the set were two light bulbs. I thought it was too good to be true; for $1000.00, something must be wrong with it, so I walked

In this world, seeing is believing, but with God, believing is seeing.

away. Then, God spoke to me to leave the store and go elsewhere.

The next day, after going elsewhere as God had commanded, I visited a different Ashley's location across town. I saw the same sofa for $800.00 —by itself. The identical loveseats were priced at $650.00, the lamps at $99.00 each, and the area rugs at $170.00. The set totaled nearly $3000.00. WHAT! I pulled a hamstring, running back to the other Ashley's store to grab my blessing. I doubted my blessing sitting on that showroom floor yesterday. And God knew my doubting spirit. I was like Doubting Thomas, thinking something was wrong with the furniture. That's why He told me to go elsewhere and price-check: to teach me a lesson about believing in Him.

Then Jesus told him, "Because you have seen me, you have believed; blessed are those who have not seen and yet have believed." John 20:27

Thankfully, God was merciful and patient. My blessing was still at the other Ashley's, waiting for me. But the lesson hadn't stopped there.

After going through my phone to call the brother who delivered my sleigh bed blessing, God directed me to get a U-Haul and do it myself. And my God, that Ashely furniture was heavy, including the end tables. It all was solid quality. My back, legs, and muscles testified to that.

I could feel God side-eyeing me, knowing I got the message: God doesn't bless people with low-quality junk.

Gentrified

During my morning prayers the following day, God said, "I gentrified you."

In my haste and ignorance, I was annoyed at the thought of being "gentrified" or made to replace my Black manhood with snootiness. I loved my culture.

He repeated it. "You are gentrified."

This time, I looked up the definition. Gentrification is making someone or something more refined, polite, or respectable. Yup, *now* that was me. After going through my faith walk, tests, and trials, I realized that the process had changed my outside surroundings and material possessions and also gentrified my inner being. I *was* new, more mature in God, richer in wisdom, and more knowledgeable of His purpose for me. At first, it appeared that my life had been turned upside down and that all hell had broken loose. However, the natural interpretation is that divine law had taken place. Divine law, or should I say, God's hand, manifesting in my life, worked towards the supreme good, even though some events appeared unfavorable to the naked eye. The apparent home loss served a greater purpose: owning my own home. Sacrifices are made for the spiritual advancement of humanity. The loss of Sandra gave me the nurturing understanding of a God-sent friend.

Consider it pure joy, my brothers and sisters, whenever you face trials of many kinds because you know that the testing of your faith produces perseverance. Let perseverance finish its work so that you may be mature and complete, not lacking anything. James 2:4

Yes, God gentrified me. And I was pleased.

He, who was seated on the throne, said, "Behold, I am making all things new." He also said, "Write this down, for these words are trustworthy and true." Revelations 21:5

So, I wrote this book.

CHAPTER 32
EPILOGUE

- WHERE I BELONG

John 10:27-28
My sheep hear My voice, and I know them, and they follow
Me. And I give them eternal life, and they shall never perish;
neither shall anyone snatch them out of My hand.

WHERE I BELONG

In the beginning, I was unclear when God told me my longing to belong was purposely put in me by Him. But now, I understand. Longing to belong roused my spirit and zeal to move through this traumatic world searching. It was the catalyst to never becoming complacent. Wherever the longing led me, or wherever God sent me, although humbling at times, I belonged there for God's purpose, which simultaneously was my purpose. I'm no longer seeking to belong. I've accepted where I belong physically, *in a new home,* and in my new mental, emotional, and spiritual space. I'm now comfortable being true to myself and being to myself. Enjoying a matinee or going out to breakfast by myself is pure heaven.

How did I get here in this space*?*

Is it "*Mind* your business" or "*Mine*" your business? (Mine, as in mining for gold) I prefer the latter.

In *mining* my business *and leaving yours alone*, I sifted out something inside me so valuable that I will no longer allow anyone to undervalue me again, including myself. That treasure is *my* story. I'm not touting myself as a prophet; I'm far from that. However, Joseph, Surah

12:111 reads: *In their (the Prophets) histories, there is certainly a lesson for men of understanding. It is not a narrative which could be forged, but a verification of what is before it, and a distinct explanation of all things, and a guide and a mercy to a people who believe.*

Our story is all we are given on this earth by The Creator. The ups and downs, the ends and outs—if we endure them with faith and overcome them, our story becomes a beacon of hope and guidance in dark times for others, but only if we accept *His* story for us and not forge our narratives. You may even make history; your story is told long after you are gone.

As I shared earlier, my story is *my* gold mine. It contains my self-worth, and I can happily say the void is finally filled. I'm soul-satisfied. I'm where I belong: squashing my beef with God and others, accepting my path, and embracing my story that is pre-written by God. To God be the glory.

THE PANTRY

Food idioms have been around for centuries, teaching and shaping us. Below are just a few that we unconsciously use.

When life serves you lemons, make lemonade.
Cold turkey.
Don't sugarcoat it.
You catch more bees with honey.
One rotten apple spoils the whole barrel.
Walking on eggshells.
Cream de la creme
You reap what you sow.
Squash the beef.

HOW MANY FOOD IDIOMS CAN YOU LIST? WRITE THEM BELOW.

YOUR FOOD IDIOMS CONTINUED.

CONSUMER ADVISORY

Nothing is more traumatic and uncomfortable than a family, co-workers, or a couple beefing at each other at home or in public.

As a chef, although I *"marry"* ingredients, meaning to put all the ingredients together and let them sit a while, I'm not a licensed couple's therapist, nor do I claim to be such. As I sought professional advice from a licensed therapist during my divorce, and when writing this book, I encourage you to pursue professional therapy regarding your relationship with yourself, your spouse, children, and others, and by all means, Squash The Beef with self, others, and God. Be obedient to Him and accept your path and purpose. Remember, out of all the billions of people, past, present, and future, God has never recycled and reused a set of fingerprints, not even yours. So, stop emulating others because your life is precisely measured for you. And you don't need to explain.

- Norma Jazz Wilson, M.Ed.,
The Restoration Counseling Center for Women
Jazz Wilson (restorationcounsellingcenter.com)

- Suicide and Crisis Lifeline - 988   Available 24 hours.

Reach out to me. I'd love to hear from you.
@Chef.terrelljabbarr

ACKNOWLEDGMENTS

All compliments are to God. He is the Author of my life. Without Him, I have no story. I thank my brothers (the Crumb-pickers) for a fantastic childhood. And indeed, thank Moses for urging me to take culinary arts. Thanks to Mr. James Mullins for directing my culinary path to College. Thanks to my brothers, Beloff, Eric, and Lew Haggler IV (RIP), for your guidance and teachings. Thanks to my brother and fellow Alumnus, Kevin James, for being certain my culinary terms were valid. I thank Gwyn of Gold Dust Editing for your direction and insightfulness. Thank you to Shirl for being a brilliant Mother and helping to shape our beautiful children into strong-willed beings. To my children, Jameel and Sasha, stay focused on your path. The grander the purpose, the longer it takes for the vision to be fulfilled. Your Grandmother/my Mom and Queen jewel, Norma Jazz Wilson, M.Ed., can attest to that. Super, thank you, Mom. Your love and therapist expertise are invaluable. Thank you for showing me that your purpose doesn't have an expiration date. Lastly, thank you, Sandra Faye, for everything. I'm thankful to God for you. You are God-sent. Rest in Peace, my Purple Queen. Cancer and pain don't live in heaven. Love you.

INDEX

www.ingramcontent.com/pod-product-compliance
Lightning Source LLC
Chambersburg PA
CBHW060506130626
46553CB00002B/417